SUPER SIMPLE
QUICK START GUIDE TO
BOOK MARKETING

ALSO BY E.J. STEVENS

Super Simple Guides

Super Simple Quick Start Guide to Self-Publishing
Super Simple Quick Start Guide to Book Marketing

Spirit Guide
Young Adult Series

She Smells the Dead
Spirit Storm
Legend of Witchtrot Road
Brush with Death
The Pirate Curse

Ivy Granger
Urban Fantasy Series

Shadow Sight
Blood and Mistletoe
Ghost Light
Club Nexus
Burning Bright
Birthright
Hound's Bite
Blood Rite (Coming 2017)
Tales from Harborsmouth (Coming 2017)

Hunters' Guild
Urban Fantasy Series

Hunting in Bruges

Dark Poetry Collections

From the Shadows
Shadows of Myth and Legend

SUPER SIMPLE
QUICK START GUIDE TO
BOOK MARKETING

E.J. Stevens

Super Simple Quick Start Guide to Book Marketing

Published by Sacred Oaks Press
Sacred Oaks, 221 Sacred Oaks Lane, Wells, Maine 04090

First Printing (trade paperback edition), January 2017

Copyright © E.J. Stevens 2016
All rights reserved

Stevens, E.J.
Super Simple Quick Start Guide to Book Marketing / E.J. Stevens

ISBN 978-1-946046-03-1 (trade pbk.)

PUBLISHER'S NOTE
This is a work of fiction. Names, characters, places, and incidents either are the product of the author's imagination or are used fictitiously, and any resemblance to actual persons, living or dead, business establishments, events, or locales is entirely coincidental.

The scanning, uploading and distribution of this book via the Internet or via any other means without the permission of the publisher is illegal and punishable by law. Please purchase only authorized electronic editions, and do not participate in or encourage electronic piracy of copyrighted materials. Your support of the author's rights is appreciated.

CONTENTS

Introduction	1
Chapter 1: Building an Author Platform	5
Chapter 2: Website and Blog	11
Chapter 3: Social Media	21
Chapter 4: Email	37
Chapter 5: Media Kit	41
Chapter 6: Creating a Marketing Plan	47
Chapter 7: Book Swag and Promotional Items	51
Chapter 8: Blog Tours, Cover Reveals, and Book Blasts	55
Chapter 9: Giveaways	61
Chapter 10: Interviews and Guest Posts	69
Chapter 11: Book Reviews and ARC Reviews	71
Chapter 12: Retail Product Pages	77
Chapter 13: SEO, Keywords, and BISAC	87
Chapter 14: Advertising and Price Promotions	95
Chapter 15: Building a Newsletter Mailing List	103
Chapter 16: Sell Sheets	107
Chapter 17: Book Signings and Conventions	109
Book Marketing Checklist	113
Book Marketing Resources	115

INTRODUCTION

Welcome to the Super Simple Quick Start Guide to Book Marketing. Whether novice or experienced writer, I hope you find this book helpful as you embark on your publishing journey. My goal is to provide you with an easy-to-follow guide that will save you time and money through tips and tricks I've developed during my writing career.

This guide is arranged in the order in which I market my own books. Each chapter will take you one step, leap, or bound closer to becoming a bestseller. Early chapters introduce concepts vital to building your author platform, and give a simple tutorial on how to complete that step, saving you valuable time. Pro tips and publishing life hacks will highlight ways to avoid common pitfalls. Later chapters provide information on what to do after your book launch, including blog tours, book signings, and running a BookBub price promotion. At the end of this guide, you'll also find a marketing checklist and a list of useful resources.

I have successfully published 15 fiction books, including the award-winning Spirit Guide young adult series, the bestselling Hunters' Guild urban fantasy series, and the award-winning, bestselling Ivy Granger, Psychic Detective urban fantasy series. In 2017, I release my first works of nonfiction, the Super Simple Quick Start Guide to Self-Publishing and this Super Simple Quick Start Guide to Book Marketing. In addition to my 2017 nonfiction releases, I will be publishing two more books in the Ivy Granger series and two books in the much anticipated Whitechapel Paranormal Society Victorian Gothic horror series.

In recent years, my books have won numerous awards. I am a BTS Red Carpet Award winner for Best Novel and Best Book Cover, SYAE finalist for Best Paranormal Series, Best Novella, and Best Horror, winner of the PRG Reviewer's Choice Award for Best Paranormal Fantasy Novel, Best Young Adult Paranormal Series, Best Urban Fantasy Novel, and finalist for

Best Young Adult Paranormal Novel and Best Urban Fantasy Series.

My novels and novellas have been translated into multiple languages, including German, Italian, Spanish, and Dutch. I have also had the pleasure of working with world famous voice artists in the production of over a half dozen audiobooks.

My books have flown to the top of the Amazon bestsellers lists in numerous categories. I have repeatedly hit the Amazon top 100, and have hit #1 in a variety of categories such as the Mythology & Folktales > Fairy Tales category and the Mystery, Thriller & Suspense > Psychics category in Amazon stores worldwide.

I have built a successful author platform with a large fan base, high visibility, and extensive media reach. My blog, From the Shadows, has received over 2.8 million page views and has an active, loyal following. On my blog, I have interviewed over 200 authors, including Faith Hunter, Darynda Jones, Joseph Nassise, Amanda Hocking, and Suzanne Johnson. I, in turn, have been interviewed by hundreds of blogs, podcasts, radio, television, and magazines, and my interviews have been translated into multiple languages. My social networks have a steady following with thousands of readers and extend across a wide range of media outlets.

I am a guest at conventions and book signings around the world. Recent conventions include Dragon Con, Boskone, Imaginarium, Readercon, and World Fantasy. I frequently speak on panels and teach workshops on a wide range of publishing, writing craft, and literary topics. I have been a guest speaker alongside such notable figures as Charles Stross, Catherynne M. Valente, Orson Scott Card, Rachel Vincent, Paul Tremblay, Maria Snyder, Leanna Renee Hieber, David Coe, Kit Reed, Peter V. Brett, Jacqueline Carey, and Max Gladstone.

It's important to remember that I did not start out as a book marketing hero. I've made mistakes, ones that you don't have to make if you follow the steps in this guide.

When I started publishing and marketing my books in 2009, there were limited resources in libraries and online. I was frustrated by conflicting information, outdated books and websites, dead links leading to 404 errors, and false information posted by people with no industry experience.

Today there are hundreds of books, videos, and websites on how to publish and market your book. This wealth of resources is great in theory, but it means that it has become more difficult to find useful information than ever before. With my years of publishing experience, I can shine a light on the most important tasks, help you set clear goals, and provide tips to ensure you achieve those goals.

The Super Simple Quick Start Guide to Book Marketing will give you the basic information needed to become a bestselling author, while providing terminology and resources that will help if you wish to learn more advanced publishing skills.

Grab your cape. It's time to be a book marketing hero!

CHAPTER 1: BUILDING AN AUTHOR PLATFORM

An author platform is a combination of your author brand and the media outlets you use to reach and connect with your audience. The goal is to create a strong author platform that builds, maintains, and grows a devoted fan base.

Why do I need an author platform? Millions of books are published each year. A strong author platform will increase your book's visibility with new readers and will guarantee sales from your established fans.

How do I build an author platform? In this chapter, we will break down the elements of your author brand and help you build your author platform. In **Chapter 2: Website and Blog** and **Chapter 3: Social Media**, I will give you the tools and information you need to successfully reach and grow your audience using free and inexpensive media outlets.

To build an author platform, you need to:
- Create an Author Brand
- Use Media Outlets to Reach Readers

Author Brand:
Whether you are self-publishing and responsible for all of your book marketing or traditionally published and looking to supplement your publisher's publicity department, it is helpful to think about your author brand.

What is an author brand? Put simply, your author brand is how you are perceived. Your author brand creates reader expectations, and those expectations can help you sell books.

How do we build an author brand? The two main building blocks of your author brand are your public persona and the books you write. Once we determine the most significant elements of your public persona and your books, we can create a memorable logo, author bio, and tagline.

Building blocks of an author brand include:
- Public Persona
- Your Books

Your public persona is the face you show to readers. Not every detail of your private life must become part of your author brand, but readers do like to get to know the person behind the books. Are you a foodie? Do you love to sniff books? Have a degree in history?

Start thinking about the details you might be willing to share with your readers as this is how they will identify with you, helping separate you from other authors. We'll explore this in more detail in the HOW TO section below.

PRO TIP: Unless your books are political, it's best to avoid controversial topics on your author media outlets. If you do share political posts, be aware that this will become part of your public persona. It is likely that some readers will be offended and not follow your social networks, no matter how much they might like to read your books.

The books you write are an important part of your author brand. Do you write in one genre or a variety of categories? Identifying the common threads between your books will give you insight into who your readers are and what they can expect from you and your writing.

Use the exercise in the HOW TO section below to explore the common themes between your books and create a powerful tagline for your author brand. A common denominator in your writing can appeal to readers across genres. Knowing the similarities between your books will improve your interactions with your audience and make it easier to write an author bio and tagline that will appeal to your fans and attract new readers.

Having one strong author brand is often better than using multiple pen names and brands, but there are exceptions. If your books are vastly different and one of your genres has the potential to offend or put off readers from your other books, then use a separate pen name.

Even if you decide to have one author brand, you may want to use a pen name. A pen name can protect your privacy, or provide ambiguity to avoid customer bias. For example, my first name is an obviously female name. When I started publishing my books seven years ago, I decided to write under E.J. Stevens to avoid potential gender bias.

Consider your audience when selecting a pen name. Whether you decide to use one pen name or multiple pen names, the name you choose can say a lot about your author brand. Does your pen name fit your genre?

If you decide to use a pen name, think about SEO (Search Engine Optimization). Can you find a way to include a genre keyword in your pen name? Does your pen name have a lot of competition? Is there another author in your genre who writes under the same name?

Researching a potential pen name by doing a Google search or searching the name on Goodreads (goodreads.com) or Amazon (amazon.com) will give you an idea of how easy it will be for readers to find you and your books. Give yourself an edge and use a unique name that will have less likelihood of reader confusion and be easier for readers to find.

PRO TIP: If one of your books or genres has the potential to offend or put off readers from your other books, use a pen name and create a separate author brand. You will need to do the exercises below for both author brands.

For example, if you write both children's books and adult romance, you will need two author brands and at least one pen name in addition to your real name or two pen names. When completing your public persona worksheets and your book worksheets in the exercise below, create one for your children's books author brand and one for your adult romance author brand. The hobbies listed and the book themes listed will be very different for each brand.

HOW TO: This exercise will help you break down the elements of your author brand to create a cohesive brand, and a logo, author bio, and tagline for your brand.

Create a public persona worksheet. Make a list of your interesting traits, specialty knowledge, and hobbies. For the initial brainstorming, do not worry about whether or not your hobbies relate to your books. The important thing is to think about topics that you are interested in and knowledgeable about.

Create a book worksheet. List all of your books. You can list both published books and works in progress.

Answer three questions about each book on your list. What is the genre category of your book? What is the theme of your book? What makes your protagonist tick? Even if your books are in different genre categories, there will often be similarities or connections between your book's themes and/or what motivates your characters.

For example, when I did a similar exercise regarding my own work, I found many common threads. No matter the genre or the age of the intended audience, I write books that tackle hard topics within the safe sandbox of fiction. All of my books and series feature strong, female protagonists who are emotionally damaged yet rise above, and always put their own necks on the line to protect the innocent. There is also a secondary theme in all of my books that asks, what truly makes a monster?

Now look over your persona worksheet and book worksheet. Do you have anything in common with your characters? Do you have a job, degree, special knowledge, or experience that relates to your books? Circle the topics on your persona worksheet that relate to your books. Cross out anything you would be embarrassed to share with the public.

Using the information on your worksheets, write a tagline for your author brand. Your tagline should be short and catchy. Try to work in keywords associated with your books. Writing a tagline for your author brand is similar to writing an elevator pitch for your novel.

A good test for your tagline is to imagine it printed on book swag such as a t-shirt or tote bag. Is your tagline memorable? Does it represent you and your books? Will your tagline fit on smaller swag items like pens and flash drives, or on a website header?

A tagline I started using when my two urban fantasy series became popular was, "bloodsucking vampires, psychotic faeries, and snarky, kick-butt heroines." At the time it was important to point out that my vampires were terrifying, not handsome and romantic, to distinguish my brand from the popular Twilight fandom. Including that there were psychotic faeries and strong, snarky heroines let readers know what kind of reading experience to expect from my books. I still incorporate that tagline into my author bio.

Try out different taglines and see what works. Run different taglines and pitches by your fans, beta readers, critique group, or author friends. Do a Google search to see if the tagline appears elsewhere. You don't want to confuse readers.

Once you decide on a tagline, think about what imagery that tagline evokes. Having a logo or iconic images for your website and social network profile headers will help convey and promote your author brand to readers.

In addition to symbols or images for your logo, you will need a font for your tagline. Fonts are typically very specific to a genre. The font you choose for your tagline should reflect your author brand.

The font you choose is important. There is a humorous meme that shows the same message printed in a curvy romantic script font and in a bloody horror font. The words (you'll always be mine) and font color (red) are the same, but the message received is very different depending on the font style.

Remember to purchase the rights to your custom font or make sure that your font is a public domain font with no licensing restrictions for commercial use, especially if you plan to use your tagline on merchandise you intend to sell.

Now that you have a concept for your author brand and a tagline for promoting that brand, you need to begin using social networking sites, websites, and blogs to establish your author brand with your audience. This is the final step in building a basic author platform.

The information in the next two chapters will help you establish your brand using social networks, a website, and/or blog. Later chapters will provide you with tips and tricks to maintain and grow your author brand and use your author platform to launch a bestseller.

CHAPTER 2: WEBSITE AND BLOG

Book marketing is about connecting with the people who are, or will become, your readers. Social media, including your website, blog, and social networking sites, is your greatest tool for making and maintaining those connections. In this chapter, we'll go over the basics of creating a website and blog. In the next chapter, **Chapter 3: Social Media**, we'll cover popular social networking sites, provide tips, tricks, and best practices for each site, and dig deeper into how to measure the effectiveness of your marketing using social media metrics.

Website:
The first step in getting your author platform online is to create an author website. You can design your own author website using sites like Wordpress, Wix, Weebly, or Squarespace, download paid design templates from sites like Etsy and CreativeMarket, or hire a professional website designer. If purchasing from Etsy, sign up with Ebates so that you get cash back on your Etsy purchase.

I highly recommend hiring a professional to design your website. Not only will a professional designer be more skilled at the actual design, they can help you navigate the process. Setting up a website is not difficult, but it can be confusing. Some sites offer hosting, some offer hosting and domain name, while others provide an integrated website builder with basic design templates and hosting. Web hosting companies provide space on a server for your website to exist and make your website accessible to the public.

Factors to consider when choosing a web host are cost, reliability, speed, security, and customer support. Popular hosting sites include HostGator (hostgator.com), BlueHost (bluehost.com), and DreamHost (dreamhost.com). Prices for website hosting can range from $60 to $200 per year.

Consulting a designer or someone fluent in web design can help you find the package best suited for your needs.

Whether you hire a professional or you design your own website, make sure to purchase a domain name that reflects your author brand. It may take a few tries to find an available domain name that matches your author brand. Don't give up. The good news is that domain names from sites like GoDaddy (godaddy.com) are inexpensive, usually costing around $10 per year.

Think of your website as an online business card. Your author website should include the following:

- Domain Name
- Header
- Author Name
- Tagline
- Home Page
- Author Page
- Book Info Page
- Social Follow Buttons
- Contact Info
- Newsletter Signup

Optional elements include:
- Appearances Page
- Media Kit/Press Page
- Link to Blog

Take what we learned about your author brand in the previous chapter and create a website that best reflects that brand. Your author brand will influence your website's color palette, background image, and header design.

Do you write sweet, clean romance with confectioner protagonists and have a reputation for giving your characters their happily ever after? You might want to use a pastel color palette, feature a cookie or coffee cup in the background image, and use a curvy script font in your header. Do you write horror and have a reputation for keeping readers awake with stories of monsters that attack their victims at night? You might want to use a dark color palette, feature a clawed hand at the window or a monstrous shape lurking in a shadowed doorway in your background image, and use an angular font in your website header.

When creating a header, include your author name in large font and your author brand tagline in a smaller font. If you have decided on a logo to go with your author brand, you can add that to your header design. Your header will display on every page of your website.

Your website should have a homepage, author page, and book page. If you have more than one series, you can have a page for each series. If you participate in book signings, book readings, or attend conventions, you can add an appearances page. I also highly recommend adding a press page with a professional media kit. Information on how to create a media kit can be found in **Chapter 5: Media Kit**.

Your author website is a landing page for your author brand. It should be clear and easy to read, should load quickly, and provide contact information and links to your blog, newsletter signup form, and your social networks.

A great way to link to your social networks is by using social follow buttons. These are buttons located either in your website's sidebar, at the top of the page, or bottom of the page, that display the logo image for each social network. Each social follow button should link to your author page on that social network. Adding social follow buttons to your website increases visibility for your social networks and extends your marketing reach.

Blog:

A blog is less formal and more interactive than your author website. Your blog is still a reflection of your author brand, so you can use the same color palette, tagline, and design elements such as your social follow buttons. Not all of your readers will come to your blog by way of your website, so make sure to include your author bio and information about your books.

It is standard for a blog to have a homepage, an about me page, a policy page, and a contact page. Provide tabs or links for each page of your blog at the top of your blog. Depending on your design, the page tabs will appear just above or just below your header.

HOMEPAGE: Your homepage is where new blog posts will appear. You want your blog to load quickly, so display only your top four or five posts. Readers can click to read more. You can also include a search box and a chronological blog post link list in the sidebar for easy navigation to older posts.

ABOUT ME: The "about me" page is where you can put your author bio and an author photo. This can be the same bio you used for your author website or you can write something less formal.

You can include information about your books on your about me page below your bio, or create a separate book page. I recommend making a separate page for your books if you've published more than three books. You don't want the page to become too cluttered, and pages with a large number of images, such as book covers, will be slower to load, leading to less satisfactory user experience.

POLICY PAGE: Most blogs include a policy page. Your policy page is where you state your blog policies and any disclaimers.

If you host giveaways on your blog, you need to state your giveaway policy on this page, such as minimum age requirements and your liability policy for prizes lost during shipping.

If you review books on your blog, you need to state your review policy on this page. State if you accept unsolicited books for review, the genres you read, and the formats you are willing to accept. Providing an estimated turnaround time for reviews is also helpful.

Don't forget to write a disclaimer if you receive any products free in exchange for an honest review, or if you use affiliate links on your blogs (see below).

Note: According to the FTC (Federal Trade Commission) guidelines, which were updated in 2009 and again in early 2016, disclosures must be made for endorsements that have received compensation and for commissions earned from affiliate links.

Reviewing a book is an endorsement. If you received a free gift card and/or a free book to review, you must disclose it. The best practice is to mention on your policy page that you sometimes receive free books in exchange for honest reviews

AND include the disclaimer in the review post on your blog. If in addition to a free book you accepted a gift card or any other form of payment, you must disclose that you received payment for your review.

If you use affiliate links on your blog (Amazon Associates, BooksAMillion, Barnes & Noble, Random House, Smashwords, IndieBound, iTunes The Book Depository), you must disclose on your policy page that you receive a commission for purchases made using the links on your blog.

CONTACT PAGE: Make it easy for readers and the press to contact you. Include a contact form, an email link, or your email address. If you hire a publicist, you can provide their name and contact information.

GETTING ONLINE: You can pay to have your website designer set up your blog when they create your author website, or you can set up a blog yourself with hosts like WordPress or Blogger.

Note: Wordpress has a free option (wordpress.com) and a self-hosted option (wordpress.org). The self-hosted option is more reliable and gives you more control and freedoms, but requires that you pay for a web hosting company. The free option of Wordpress limits your ability to alter the template and customize plugins.

Even if you decide to use a free blog site, you will want to purchase a premade or custom design template from blog designers like Parajunkee Designs or NoseGraze. You will also need to select and purchase a domain name for your blog.

At the time of writing this, Blogger has an integrated system for purchasing a blog domain through GoDaddy without leaving the Blogger dashboard. Go to **Settings**, click on **Basic**, and go to **Publishing**. The GoDaddy domain registration costs about $10 per year, and users have the option to buy their own domain on their own and add it to their Blogger dashboard settings. The free WordPress site (wordpress.com) charges $18 per year for a domain registration through WordPress. WordPress users who want to choose their own domain company, and save money on domain registration, have to use premium Wordpress (wordpress.org).

The major difference between your author website and your blog is that readers can comment on your blog posts. You will need to make sure in your blog settings that post comments are allowed. You also need to decide if you want to use the default comment system that comes with your blog or install a third-party comment system like Disqus, IntenseDebate, LiveFyre, or Google+ Comments. Factors to consider for your comment system are ease of use and spam protection.

Comment spam is an unsolicited commercial message left as a comment on your blog. You can control spam with comment moderation, require clicking a checkbox to demonstrate that the commenter is not a robot, or by using CAPTCHA.

Comment moderation requires you to read and approve each comment before it becomes visible to the public. You can select to have notifications sent to your email, or you can manually check your blogging dashboard to check for and approve comments. Checking a box to demonstrate you are not a robot is self explanatory, but you can be creative and change the wording from robot to vampire or werewolf, for example. CAPTCHA is effective, but is the most annoying for your readers. CAPTCHA requires typing in the letters and/or numbers shown on the screen or solving a puzzle, which can be difficult and time consuming.

While spam is annoying to the blogger, consider your readers first. If you make it too difficult for readers to comment on your blog, you may miss out on interacting with potential fans. Conversely, if your blog is being inundated by pornographic, violent, or otherwise upsetting comment spam, adding an extra layer of spam protection will prevent readers from becoming offended and leaving your blog. Decisions about spam protection must be made on a case-by-case basis and can change over time.

For example, I had one week where I received thousands of spam messages. I added comment moderation and deleted the spam messages. The following month, I removed comment moderation, but the spam did not increase. The spam system targeting my blog had realized that my blog was no longer an easy target and moved on.

When setting up a new blog, I recommend not turning on advanced spam protection. Monitor your blog comments. If spam becomes a problem, experiment with using one of the spam protection methods for a week. Are you losing readers? Are less readers interacting? If you turn the spam protection off, does the spam increase again? Find the method that works best for you and your readers.

Note: Another design option is to make your blog available as a page of your author website. Check with your website designer regarding potential benefits and limitations of merging your website and blog.

BLOGGING: Your blog is online, now what? In order for your blog to be successful, and for you to build a strong author platform, you need to build, maintain, and grow your blog audience.

There are four elements that are essential for a successful blog. You must:
- Post Frequently
- Provide Interesting Content
- Promote Content
- Interact

The most popular frequency is to post 2 to 5 blog posts per week. Search engines rank sites higher if they update frequently, and fresh content keeps readers interested and engaged. But you will need to experiment with a blog posting schedule that works for you.

I built a large audience for my blog, From the Shadows (fromtheshadows.info), gaining over 2.8 million page views and receiving over 10 thousand comments, by posting 3 times per week for 7 years. I struggled to maintain this posting rate while on tour in 2015, but it wasn't until 2016 that I had to reduce my post frequency due to obligations while on another world book tour. My goal for 2017 is to find a new balance between writing deadlines, tour dates, and social media, and return to posting to my blog at least 2 times per week.

It is not enough to post frequently. You need to write interesting blog posts with engaging headlines. If content is boring, your blog will have a high bounce rate. Put simply, bounce rate is the percentage of visitors to your site who quickly leave the site. A high bounce rate is bad. Your homepage design and blog post titles should grab visitors, and the post content should keep them reading, commenting, and clicking within your site.

You must post diverse quality content. Popular blog post types include book reviews, book news, event recaps, "shelfies" (photos of your bookshelf or new books you've recently bought), and giveaways.

A common pitfall authors stumble into is only writing about their own books. Talk about other books you've recently read and genre related TV shows and movies you've watched. Let your personality, and your author brand, shine. You can relate things to your books without ever giving a hard sell. Have a character that is addicted to baking? Why not share some of your favorite recipes on your blog?

Another way to diversify content and bring new readers to your blog is invite other authors and bloggers to your blog. Author interviews and guest posts are a great way to help promote another author and to encourage their readers to stop by your blog. Write up a set of questions or post topics and contact authors or bloggers you think would be a good fit with your readers.

Blog hops, sometimes called link-ups, are also a fun way to encourage bloggers to visit and comment on your blog. Participate in an established blog hop or set up one of your own. Bloggers can add their blogs to the hop easily with widgets like Linky Tools, SimplyLinked, Mister Linky, and InLinkz. If setting up your own blog hop, keep in mind that some of the linking tools require a paid subscription.

The goal of a blog hop is for every blogger to visit, follow, and comment on every participating blog. Blog hops are a great way to increase the number of visitors and blog followers.

Note: Add a widget like GFC (Google Friend Connect), Bloglovin', G+ follow button, or the Wordpress follow button to give your readers a way to follow your blog. You can also add a subscribe widget, giving readers a way to subscribe to blog posts by email.

If you want to participate in more blog hops, look for active blog memes. What's a blog meme? When blog hops happen on a regular schedule, they're often referred to as memes. The memes that are active and popular change over time, but usually run on a set weekly schedule. Current memes include Mailbox Monday, Top Ten Tuesday, Waiting on Wednesday, TBR Thursday, Friday 56, Saturday Review of Books, and the Sunday Post. Every blog hop has different rules, so read the instructions before posting.

PRO TIP: A great way to increase blog traffic and invite discussion is to visit other blogs and interact with the book blogging community. Find book blogs that focus on your genre, read through recent posts, and leave a comment. NEVER try to sell your books in a blog comment, and NEVER make a negative comment on a review of one of your books. Be thoughtful and considerate and have fun! Let your personality shine through and you'll quickly become a part of the book blogging community.

CHAPTER 3: SOCIAL MEDIA

When creating your author brand, you defined your audience. In order to choose the most effective social media sites for your author platform, pay attention to your audience and where they hang out online.

Facebook is often a safe bet with over 1 billion users, but it's helpful to expand your reach by using additional social media sites that target your readers. If, for example, you write young adult books, you might want to try one of the networks like YouTube or SnapChat that is popular with a younger crowd. Do you have a fashion obsessed protagonist? If you've incorporated fashion into your book marketing, you'll want to focus on image-centric social media like Pinterest, Twitter, Flickr, and Instagram.

Leveraging the power of social media requires a flexible marketing strategy and an investment of time. Social media trends change rapidly, so reevaluate your marketing plan quarterly. A social networking platform that works for connecting and engaging with readers today might not be as effective next month or next year.

In this chapter, we'll cover popular social networking sites, provide tips, tricks, and best practices for each site, and dig deeper into how to measure the effectiveness of your marketing using social media metrics.

Twitter: Twitter is a free social networking site that forces users to be concise by limiting each post or "tweet" to 140 characters or less. As of September 2016, images no longer count toward the 140-character limit. This form of micro-blogging has become popular and Twitter now has over 300 million users.

PRO TIP: Twitter will automatically shorten URLs that you put into a tweet. You can also use a URL shortener like Bitly, TinyURL, Buffer, or Hootsuite to add links to your tweets that do not put your message over the 140 character limit, but if you do not need to track your URLs, the best shortener is the one built into Twitter. If using an alternate shortener, keep in mind that some users might assume the link is spam.

A Twitter language has evolved due to the site format and the character limit. Twitter terms you need to know are:
- Tweet
- Retweet (RT)
- Avatar
- Handle (@name)
- Mention
- Direct Message (DM)
- Hashtag (#hashtag)

Twitter has a bird for its logo, which is a great way to remember Twitter micro conversations are referred to as tweets (birds make that "tweet tweet" sound). A tweet is an individual message post. To retweet (RT) is to share a post to your feed. This is similar to sharing on Facebook. You can retweet a post by clicking the retweet button, or by beginning a tweet with the letters RT and copying and pasting the original tweet and clicking the tweet button.

Your Twitter avatar is the photo associated with your account. For authors, this can be your logo, author photo, protagonist's photo, or newest book cover image. Never leave your avatar blank. The Twitter avatar default is an egg. This indicates that you're a newbie. Get it? The egg indicates a new, baby bird. Make sure to check how your avatar looks on a computer screen and on your phone screen. 80% of Twitter users access Twitter on a mobile device.

While updating your avatar to match your author brand, include an author bio. Your Twitter bio has a 160 character limit, so this will be much shorter than the bio you put on your website and blog. Include your publishing highlights, such as "award-winning author of" or "NYT bestselling author of" and give the book or series.

Twitter handles have a 15 character limit, 16 if you count the @ symbol. It's best to use the shortest handle possible, to make it easier to be added to a tweet, while remaining true to your author brand. Try to keep your username as similar as you can for all sites within your author platform.

For example, my Twitter handle is @EJStevensAuthor (feel free to come follow me on Twitter!). It was necessary to add author to my name due to a sports celebrity with the same name. For the sake of consistency, my email uses "E.J.Stevens.Author" and my official website is www.EJStevensAuthor.com.

Each Twitter user has a handle beginning with the @ symbol. A Twitter handle is the way that Twitter users identify you in messages (tweets). Including someone's Twitter handle in a tweet is meant to tag that person's Twitter account and get their attention.

We use the term mention when we talk about a Twitter user's handle being included in a tweet. To mention someone is to add their handle, their Twitter username, to the conversation. Here is an example:

I just gave SHADOW SIGHT by @EJStevensAuthor a 5-star review on @Goodreads.

In this example, the user mentioned two accounts. You can mention as many accounts in a tweet as you want so long as you remain within the 140 character limit.

PRO TIP: Tweets that begin with the @ symbol are only visible to that person and mutual friends. The tweet is not visible to the public.

A frequent mistake new Twitter users make is to begin a tweet with someone's Twitter handle thinking they are just mentioning that person. Here is an example:

@EJStevensAuthor is on my blog today discussing the Top 5 spookiest places in Bruges, Belgium.

In the example above, the tweet would not show on the blogger's Twitter feed and they would be missing the opportunity to promote the blog post. You and the blogger, and mutual friends, would be the only ones to see this tweet. This can easily be remedied by placing a period in front of the @ symbol.

.@EJStevensAuthor will be at the signing event at the Haverhill Public Library this weekend!

This example will be public and visible to all users.

If you begin a tweet with someone's Twitter handle, only that person and mutual friends (people who follow BOTH you and the other person's Twitter account) will see it. If you want the discussion to be visible to all users, put a period in front of the @ symbol.

In addition to mentions, you can send a direct message (DM) to Twitter users. Direct messages are private messages and, depending on the user's settings, may prompt an email alert that they have a new DM waiting to be read. Use this feature sparingly.

PRO TIP: Do not abuse Twitter DMs. Never send a DM trying to sell or promote your books.

Hashtags are a word or phrase preceded by the pound sign (#). Hashtags automatically become hyperlinked and searchable on Twitter. The three most popular ways to use hashtags on Twitter is to indicate a keyword or conversation topic, a live Twitter chat or party, or to add emphasis. Here are examples of the three popular ways to use hashtags on Twitter:

HOUND'S BITE the new #IvyGranger series #urbanfantasy by @EJStevensAuthor is out now!

HOUND'S BITE by @EJStevensAuthor is out now! Come join the #HBchat #HBparty and win prizes.

HOUND'S BITE by @EJStevensAuthor is out now! #releaseday #bookbirthday #omg #muppetflail

In the first example, the hashtags are related to a book series and genre. The hashtags are not time sensitive and the topics can be followed and the tweet read at any time. In the second example, the hashtags indicate a time-sensitive live chat party. Twitter users can click on the party or chat hashtags to follow and participate in the conversation. In the third example, the hashtags are used for emotional emphasis to draw attention to the book's release day and the author's excitement. Popular hashtags for readers and writers are included in the Instagram PRO TIP later in this chapter.

Now that you know the basics, it's time to build a Twitter following. Follow influencers, preferably authors, publishers, and book bloggers. Influencers have a large following and they receive a high number of interactions, such as likes, retweets, and mentions. If you are having difficulty finding influencers, you can look at sites like Klout (klout.com) and Crowdfire (crowdfireapp.com) that can suggest influencers to follow.

Just like with your blog, you need to create interesting content and post frequently. The good thing is that you can use your Twitter account to drive traffic to your blog. Use a snappy headline with the link and you're also adding content to your Twitter.

Don't forget that Twitter is social media. Social media is part of our book marketing strategy, but do not tweet frequently about your books.

PRO TIP: Use a social media assistant like Tweetdeck, Hootesuite, or Buffer to monitor your social media campaigns and schedule tweets. I always use Tweetdeck when hosting a Twitter chat or party. You can add a column to your Tweetdeck dashboard for watching all activity on your chat or party hashtag, and it refreshes in real time.

Instagram: Instagram is a visual, image-centric social media site where users post, share, and comment on photos. Book covers are photos, so go ahead and post your book covers. Keep your photos interesting and try to get creative. Following the hashtag #bookstagram is a great way to get ideas.

Inspirational quotes and book quotes are also popular on Instagram (and on Twitter). You can easily create quote photos using sites like Quozio or Canva. Quote from your books, find inspirational quotes, and quote famous authors.

If you're looking for inspiration, search the quote database on Goodreads. Visit **Goodreads** (goodreads.com), move your cursor to the **Community** tab, and select **Quotes** from the drop down menu. You can find quotes by author or keyword by entering text into the search bar at the top of the page and clicking the **Search** button.

PRO TIP: Use hashtags to increase your Instagram traffic. Popular hashtags for writers and for readers are #amwriting, #amediting, #AuthorsofInstagram, #books, #bookstagram #FridayReads, #FF, (or #FollowFriday), #IndieAuthors, #LitChat, #MustRead, #NaNoWriMo (National Novel Writing Month), #TeaserTuesday, #WritersofInstagram, and #WW (or #WriterWednesday). These hashtags are also popular on Twitter!

YouTube: YouTube is a social site for sharing videos. Creating video content, adding it to your YouTube profile, and sharing the YouTube links on social media sites like Twitter and on your blog can be a great way to promote your books and your author brand.

Book trailers, like movie trailers but to promote your books, are popular. You can hire a professional to make your trailers, or make your own.

Video interviews and chats are also popular. Let your readers know that you'll be doing a video interview, and ask them to send in their questions.

Have a hobby, especially one related to your books or characters? Let your personality shine through and make a video of you playing the ukulele, telling jokes, or baking sugar cookies shaped like your characters.

Need inspiration? Follow popular booktubers and vloggers and discover the current popular trends.

PRO TIP: Be aware, because of the increasingly volatile conflict between Facebook and Youtube, if you share Youtube links on your Facebook page, your reach to fans will dramatically decrease.

Pinterest: Pinterest is visually oriented like Instagram, but is less social than other social media sites. Users can create a profile and boards for their pins. Pins are pinned images from around the internet, and boards are virtual pin boards or bulletin boards. You can also follow other profiles and boards, and like, share, save, and comment on pinned images. Although engagement happens on Pinterest, commenting happens less often than on most other social media sites. Do not worry if you do not receive many comments on your Pinterest boards.

The best practices for using Pinterest as an author are to set up a business account with a profile that matches your author brand and to create themed boards for your books, book series, or genre. If you have a blog, make a board for your blog where you can pin all images and book covers featured in your blog posts.

PRO TIP: Choosing to use a Pinterest business account will give you access to analytics. With Pinterest analytics, you'll be able to monitor impressions, clicks, and repins.

You can begin pinning images to a board before your book is even done. Readers love themed boards that show your writing, character, or world building inspiration. If you have celebrities in mind when creating your characters, consider making a Pinterest board for movie and TV stars you'd hypothetically cast for bringing the book to film.

PRO TIP: Install the Pin It button widget to your blog to easily pin from your blog to Pinterest. Once installed (installation varies by blogging platform), select Image Hover in the settings. This way the Pinterest save button will appear every time someone hovers over any image on your blog, providing a reminder and an easy point and click way for visitors, and you, to pin your blog images to Pinterest boards.

Note that the widget, or an abundance of plugins, may slow down some websites. Do a speed test. If you have speed issues, you can install the Pinterest plugin into any browser and it turns every image on any website into a pinnable image you can instantly share.

LinkedIn: If your website is like an online business card, then LinkedIn is your online resume. You can think of LinkedIn like a Facebook for professionals. LinkedIn is not as actively social as other social media sites, but it's still worth creating and maintaining an account. If you want more social interaction on LinkedIn, join one of the thousands of LinkedIn groups.

LinkedIn is geared toward building and maintaining your professional network. Your profile visitors for LinkedIn will be a different mix from your other social media sites. There is less emphasis on readers and more emphasis on connecting with professionals in your industry such as bloggers, authors, publishers, publicists, editors, cover designers, translators, and narrators.

Create a professional profile with a great tagline, use your author photo for your profile photo, and include your educational, work, and publishing highlights. Make sure to complete your profile. Self-publishing has lost most of its former stigma, but there are still some industry professionals who look down on self-published authors. If you're self-published or hybrid published, a great LinkedIn profile can help to legitimize you and your writing. A professional LinkedIn profile can also help when looking for a publishing, film, audio, or translation contract.

Begin to build LinkedIn connections by connecting with professionals you already know. Sending out connection request to bloggers, editors, cover designers, and author you know will help to build your initial network, and the lack of rejections will keep you from being flagged as a spammer.

You can connect with me on my LinkedIn page (www.linkedin.com/in/e-j-stevens-b0a63016). It usually takes me 48 hours to approve new requests.

Professionals who know you are also more likely to give you endorsements on your profile page. Once you've created a profile and network and gained endorsements, you can reach out to industry professionals to grow your network.

PRO TIP: Since LinkedIn is less social, it's easy to forget about. Make a calendar note to return and update your profile quarterly. Add any new accomplishments such as books published and awards won.

Facebook: Facebook is the most popular social media site with over 1 billion users. There are multiple ways to incorporate Facebook into your author platform and to utilize Facebook as part of your book marketing strategy.

Facebook can be divided into the following sections:
- Personal Profile
- Professional Pages
- Groups
- Events
- Advertising

It's important to remember that each area within Facebook comes with its own set of rules and limitations. Knowing the major pitfalls will keep your marketing on track and help you stay out of Facebook jail, a common term for Facebook limiting your access to posting, commenting, or logging in due to abuse. I'll give an overview of each area of Facebook below with the tips and tricks to make Facebook work for you.

Personal Profile: The first decision authors need to make is whether to use a personal profile, an author page, or both. A Facebook profile is a personal account for non-commercial use and lacks the business and marketing tools built into Facebook pages. A personal profile post is, however, more likely to be seen in the Facebook newsfeed and is a more likely place for friendly interactions and post engagement. On the downside, a personal profile is limited to 5,000 friends.

You need to be aware that for personal profiles, Facebook insists on using your real, legal name. If you are writing under a pen name, you need to use a professional page. If your legal name and author name are the same, I recommend maintaining a personal profile and at least one Facebook page.

I use my personal profile for interacting with author friends, publishing industry friends, and my top fans. I deny most friend requests, which is where my author page comes in handy. My author page is for sharing less personal information and more focused on book releases, giveaways, and tour dates. I also maintain a Facebook page for my blog where I cross post the headline and link to each new blog post.

Time is a concern. While some content can be posted across multiple sites, you will need to make the time to create content specific to your profile and your specific pages. Consider your writing schedule and the time allotted for your other book marketing tasks when deciding on how much Facebook real estate to commit to.

PRO TIP: Whether trying to increase visibility for your posts from a personal profile or professional page, add video content. Facebook is trying to overtake YouTube as the top video platform. As part of that strategy, Facebook is making posts with Facebook video content (not YouTube videos) more visible in the newsfeed. At the moment, over 8 billion videos are viewed on Facebook daily.

Professional Pages: Facebook pages can be used in various ways to promote your author brand, your books, and your blog. You can set up multiple pages, such as an author page, book or series page, or blog page.

The downside of professional pages is that they are only visible to users who like your page. For this reason, make sure to add a link to your Facebook page(s) on your website, blog, and newsletter. You can send invites to friends from your personal page, but be cautious. Do not spam your friend's list. Be selective about who you invite, and only send an invitation to like your page once.

Even if a person likes your page, at this time there is only about a 33% chance that your post will appear in their feed. The best ways to increase this percentage is to create quality content that readers are likely to engage with or by paying to boost or promote the post. The more readers engage with your post, and how quickly they engage, will increase the number of fans that see a page post.

A helpful feature available on page posts, but not on profile posts, is the ability to schedule out your posts. Find the time when you're the most likely to get engagement with your readers and schedule your posts for that time of day. But if you automate your posts, don't forget to visit your page to reply to comments and interact with your page's readers.

Engagement such as likes, shares, and comments help drive newsfeed visibility, but Facebook is a business and wants you to pay to promote your business content. The cost to boost or promote a post depends on the desired reach.

When setting up an author page, make sure that your header and profile photo match your author brand. Add your author bio and links to your website and blog to your author page. If you create a page for a specific series, make sure to update the header and profile image when you have a new book release in that series.

PRO TIP: Facebook pages offer a call-to-action button. Add a newsletter signup button to your Facebook page(s) to grow your mailing list. Select sign up as the type of call-to-action button, or you can add the button from your newsletter service site (for integrated sites) such as Mailchimp. If adding the button through Mailchimp, you need to setup Facebook integration first. Check Mailchimp Help for more information on this.

Groups: Facebook groups are a place to discuss a specific topic. You need to join a group in order to be able to post to the group.

Be considerate, do not spam by posting too frequently, and always read the group's posting rules. Sometimes the group topic is book promotion, and some groups encourage self-promotion, but don't assume that promotion is okay. Each group has their own set of rules, so make sure to check the top "pinned" post, the about section, and the files section before posting. Violating the rules can quickly get you banned from a group.

Facebook groups can be open, secret, or closed. An open group is open and visible to the public. A secret group can't be seen by anyone who isn't a member. A closed group and its members are visible, but group posts are only visible to members.

Open groups that allow promotion can be a good place to announce a new release or a limited time price promotion. There are even Facebook groups dedicated to genre specific promotions such as 99 cent deals and new audiobook release announcements. Even if they invite promotion, make sure to follow the rules regarding how often a specific book can be mentioned or author can post.

Another concern is ending up in Facebook jail for posting too often to groups. This is a new automated function to help prevent spam. Use caution and limit your posts to no more than ten posts per hour and twenty posts per day. Changing the post text so that each post is not identical is also recommended.

Events: The two most popular ways for authors to use Facebook events is for promoting a live, real life event or for hosting a Facebook party.

Real life events include book signings, readings, and convention appearances. Larger events like conventions will have their own event page. Select "going" to let people know you will be attending the event. This will also default to sending you notifications of new posts on the event page. You can also select "add event to page" and the event will appear on your page for fans to see. If creating your own Facebook event page, make sure to include the event name, location, time, admission fee, and any additional admission requirements such as age or membership.

Facebook events can also be used for virtual parties. Parties are often to celebrate something specific like a new book release. A popular party format is for multiple authors to participate, and each author is scheduled for a party takeover hour. During that hour the author will post to the event page, interacting with readers, playing games, and typically giving away prizes such as books, gift cards, and signed swag.

You can host your own Facebook party or participate in another author or publisher's party. No matter who is in charge, make sure that no one is breaking Facebook's rules regarding giveaways and promotions.

You must include a statement at the bottom of each giveaway post releasing Facebook of any responsibility and letting entrants know the promotion is in no way sponsored, endorsed or administered by, or associated with, Facebook. You must also include the promotion's official rules clearly stating who is eligible to enter. You cannot ask entrants to share your page on their timeline or a friend's timeline to enter.

Facebook frequently changes their terms of service. Be sure to check the most current rules before posting a giveaway to your author page or an event page.

When running giveaways, keep in mind all local regulations and retailer rules. For example, it is against Amazon's terms of service (TOS) to make posting a book review an entry option in a giveaway. This is considered paying the reviewer for the giveaway.

PRO TIP: When creating a Facebook event, you must choose whether to have the event page be public or private. You CAN NOT CHANGE THIS SETTING once the group is created.

Advertising: In addition to being a social media site, Facebook also offers multiple advertising options. You can boost posts from your professional pages and run a variety of targeted ads. Since this chapter is on social media, we'll cover Facebook ads later in **Chapter 14: Advertising and Price Promotions**.

Keep in mind that the Facebook algorithm for visibility and organic reach is constantly changing. Boosting a post might work today, but with Facebook being the largest social media site it's worth watching for trends. Talk with other authors in your genre and read monthly articles to see what is working, and not working, at the moment. In the end, the best way to make your posts visible on Facebook's newsfeed is to create interesting content that your readers are likely to engage (comment, like, share) with.

PRO TIP: Facebook is arguably your most important social media site. To improve visibility and engagement on Facebook, only post your top performing posts to Facebook.

Test your post topics on your other networks first. Post that clever inspirational quote, joke, or bit of book news on Twitter and see how well it performs. If it does not receive a good number of likes, shares, or replies, don't post it to Facebook.

Social Media Metrics:

Social media metrics are data and statistics that can help you measure your social media marketing performance. You can measure the effectiveness of your social media marketing strategy, and individual social media campaigns, with these basic social media metrics:
- Page Likes (Follows, Friends)
- Reach (Visits, Impressions, Mentions)
- Engagement (Clicks, Likes, Comments, Shares, Replies)

A simple way to think of these three social media metrics is that we're looking at your overall audience, how many eyes looked at your social media pages and posts at any given timeframe, and how much did those visitors interact while they were there. The goal is to grow a large audience of followers who frequently visit your social media pages and continually engage through clicks, likes, comments, replies, and shares.

Each social media site provides this data within the user dashboard. If you prefer to save time and have all of your data in one place, you can use a social media management site like Crowdfire, Buffer, or Sprout Social to monitor and display your social media metrics all in one dashboard. Sprout costs $59-$500 per month, Hootsuite costs $9.99-$99.99 per month, and Buffer costs $99-$399 per month for a plan that includes analytics. Crowd Booster costs $9-$119 per month, but only provides analytics for Facebook and Twitter.

PRO TIP: Follow your social media metrics to see patterns related to holidays and the time of year, month, week, or day. Find the times when you have the best audience reach and engagement and schedule important posts during those times.

Is the ideal posting time an inconvenient time for you to be on your phone or computer? Facebook pages and blogging sites like Blogger allow scheduling in the post options. Need to post to your other social media sites? Use post scheduling tools like Tweetdeck, Hootsuite, Sprout Social, SocialOomph, or Buffer to schedule your posts.

Setting up your posts with post schedulers means no more worrying about sleeping late, getting stuck in a meeting, losing internet connection, your phone battery running low, getting sick, or forgetting to make an important post on time. No matter what life throws at you, your important posts will post when you need them to.

CHAPTER 4:
EMAIL

Setting up your author email is an important part of building your author platform. Your email address and email signature say a lot about you. Use a professional, easy to remember email address that matches your author brand and an informative email signature that includes your name and links to your website and social media sites.

Sounds easy, right? This is an area where I made an early misstep. It's easy to make a mistake and difficult, and costly, to change later.

In my case, I created a Gmail address with my author name. While not terrible, I should have secured a domain name for my author site and matched my email to that. Now, eight years later, that author email address is printed on business cards and postcards, is in all of my professional contact's address books, and linked on hundreds of sites. Changing to a more effective email address now requires the cost of reprinting materials and diligently checking that mail is forwarding. Learn from my mistake. It's much easier to change your email address early in your writing career.

Having an email address such as, daboyz9999@gmail.com will quickly give away the level of professionalism. Appearances mean everything. While authorname@gmail.com is better, it would be even more effective to have name@authorwebsite.com which also helps inform people you have an author website. It's a subtle way to repeat information without constantly saying, "visit my site."

PRO TIP: If changing from a Gmail address to a domain address, you can now upgrade your free Gmail account to a business account. This requires a monthly subscription fee and a Google Apps for Work registration, but can make for an easier transition.

Email Address:

Choose an email address that matches your author brand and is easy to remember. Do not use numbers and contractions. The ideal author email will match your author brand and end in your website domain name.

If you can't afford an email address, create a Gmail account. It's not as professional as using your domain name, but Gmail is a trusted site with a great track record for reliable up time. Do not use Yahoo or Hotmail.

PRO TIP: We'll cover creating a mailing list and author newsletter later in the book, but keep in mind that some mailing services, such as Mailchimp, will no longer allow you to send your newsletter from Gmail, Yahoo, or Hotmail email addresses. This is one more reason to go with a dot com style of email address based on your author website domain name.

You may be wondering if you can use your existing email. If so, check that it doesn't make one of the classic mistakes. The most common pitfalls are:
• Misspellings and Contractions - eejaystevens@email.com
   • Shared Account - thestevensfamily@email.com
   • Sexy/ Flirty - sexystevens@email.com
   • Nonsensical - wutuppixiegal@email.com
   • Numbers - ejstevens1234@email.com

Even if your books are flirty or your characters use a lot of text message shorthand, don't make these email address blunders. Remember that you are running a business. If your email does not look professional, you may miss out on opportunities. Even worse, if your email address is a collection of nonsensical characters or includes numbers, it may never make it past your reader's and colleague's spam filter.

Email Signature:

Leverage the power of your email signature. Remind or let people know who you are, what you do, and what you have to offer. At a minimum, include your name and a link to you website. I also include links to my most active social media sites.

An email signature can be as simple or as fancy as you want. Simple text is fine, but there are many options if you'd like to make your signature more colorful or include an author photo or book cover photos and social follow buttons. The easiest way to add a fancy signature is by using an email signature tool, sometimes called email signature generators, like WiseStamp (wisestamp.com) or ZippySig (zippysig.com).

Even if you use a signature tool for a more advanced, fancy signature, try not to go overboard. Think of your email signature like a digital business card. A signature that is too large, flashy, or contains too much information will look unprofessional. Keep your signature design clean and easy to read.

PRO TIP: Social links in your email signature can increase your social reach as much as 10%. The most popular social media links to include are Facebook and Twitter.

CHAPTER 5: MEDIA KIT

Now that you've built an author platform, it's time to create a media kit. A media kit, or press kit, is a collection of information and images that any member of the press (newspaper reporter, magazine writer, TV host, radio host, book blogger) might need in order to report about you or your books.

A general media kit for you and your books, which I call an author media kit, should be linked to your website and blog. You can also include links on social media sites. Event specific media kits, such as for an online cover reveal or in-person book release party, can be included when responding to bloggers who signed up for a blog tour event or event coordinators at your host venue.

AUTHOR MEDIA KIT: The purpose of an author media kit is to make it easy for the press to contact you and report about you and your books. Having a media kit available helps enable free publicity. Make your media kit easy to use, and provide everything the press might need.

Essentials for an author media kit include:
- Author Photo
- Author Bio
- Contact Info
- Social Media Links

Optional materials to include:
- Writing Resume
- Press Releases
- Interviews
- Biblio Bio
- Book Covers

- Sell Sheets
- Book Excerpts
- Link to Reviews

At a minimum, your media kit needs your author bio, contact information, and links to all of your social media sites. If you have an agent or publicist, include their contact information as well.

It will take an investment of time, but I recommend writing an author resume specific to your writing career. As with any resume, try to keep it to a maximum of two pages, put your name and contact information at the top of the page, and organize the information into categories. For my writing resume, I use experience, publications, public speaking, blogging, education, awards, and achievements as my categories, and I only include what is relevant to my writing career.

Press releases and interviews are a great resource for members of the press interested in you and your books. Press releases are sound bites written with the press in mind. A press release might give your site's visitor an idea for a story or headline. Your past interviews are also a useful reference that can give the press an idea of what kinds of questions to ask you and demonstrate how well you perform in written, audio, and video interviews. Provide a sample of recent written (blog, newspaper, magazine), audio (radio, podcast), and video (booktubes, vlogs, television) interviews in your media kit.

In addition to the author basics, I like to have plenty of information about my books in my media kit. I want to make it easy for book reviewers, bloggers, the press, libraries, and book stores to know more about my books. For this reason, I include a biblio bio, book covers, sell sheets, book excerpts, and links to reviews.

Want to learn how to create sell sheets for your books? We cover the how and why of sell sheets in **Chapter 16: Bookstores, Libraries, and Sell Sheets**. While I rarely see authors include these in their media kits, sell sheets are a powerful book marketing tool. Because physical sell sheets can be expensive to produce and mail out, digital sell sheets are a great alternative. And if you've decided to invest in physical copies, you'll already have the digital file. If you create sell sheets, do include them in your media kit.

I also rarely see authors include more than a basic author bio. While an author bio is vital, going a step further and adding a biblio bio is important if you've written more than one book or have won a large number of book awards. A biblio bio gives the highlights of your book achievements in chronological order, often with novels first, then short fiction and poetry.

Here is an example of a biblio bio I used in early 2016:

E.J. Stevens' tenth novel Birthright (Sacred Oaks, 2015) won the BTS Red Carpet Award for Best Novel and the PRG Reviewer's Choice Award for Best Urban Fantasy Novel. The Ivy Granger series was a PRG Reviewer's Choice Award finalist for Best Urban Fantasy Series, is a SYAE Award finalist for Best Paranormal Series, and is available in multiple languages. In addition to Birthright, the series includes Hound's Bite (2016), Burning Bright (2015), Ghost Light (2014), and Shadow Sight (2012) winner of the PRG Reviewer's Choice Award for Best Paranormal Fantasy Novel. The Hunters' Guild series, which includes Hunting in Bruges (2014), is set in the same fantasy world as the Ivy Granger series. In addition to her adult fiction, E.J. wrote the humorous, young adult Spirit Guide series. The five novel series (2010-2013) won the PRG Reviewer's Choice Award for Best Young Adult Paranormal Series, and includes Brush with Death (2012) winner of the PRG Reviewer's Choice Award for Best Young Adult Paranormal Novel.

Her short fiction includes two Ivy Granger novellas, Club Nexus (2013) and Blood and Mistletoe (2012) a SYAE Award finalist for Best Novella and Best Horror. She has also written two collections of poetry, Shadows of Myth and Legend (2010) and From the Shadows (2009).

When E.J. isn't at her writing desk, she enjoys dancing along seaside cliffs, singing in graveyards, and sleeping in faerie circles. E.J. currently resides in a magical forest on the coast of Maine where she finds daily inspiration for her writing.

If you have a biblio bio in your media kit, make sure to update it to reflect new publishing accomplishments. Bring immediate attention to recent awards won by leading with those awards in the opening sentence.

PRO TIP: Add a calendar reminder to alert you to update your media kit. The frequency of updates will depend on your individual writing and publishing speed. If you publish annually, set an alert for the end of each calendar year. If you publish multiple books each year, set alerts to coincide with your book releases.

EVENT MEDIA KIT: If you plan to participate in online blog events or in-person book release parties for your books, you will need event specific media kits. You can create your own or hire someone to create your event media kit for you.

If you hire a publicist or blog tour company to run your events, they may include the creation and/or distribution of your event media kit as part of their services. Make sure to ask if a media kit is included before paying for a PR package.

An event media kit is specific to the event, but will still include some of the information you used above in your author media kit. Your event media kit will differ depending on if the event is happening online or in-person.

VIRTUAL EVENT: A media kit for an online event needs to provide bloggers with everything they need to create a blog post.

A virtual event media kit should include:
- Author Photo
- Author Bio
- Social Media Links
- Contact Info
- Book Cover
- Book Description
- Release Date
- Purchase Links
- Event Date
- Event Banner/Button*
- Post HTML*
- Book Excerpt*
- Giveaway*

As with any media kit, include your author bio, author photo, social media links, and contact information. If you're using a PR company to run your event, make that clear in any correspondence with bloggers and include the company's contact information.

Provide book details such as the book cover, description, release date, and purchase links. If the book is in a series, provide the series name and the book's location in the series.

PRO TIP: Name your photos such as your book cover, author photo, or event banner images files clearly and add your top keywords. This will make the files easy for participants to find and use, and will improve each post's performance with search engines.

An in-person event media kit needs to provide the venue and attendees with the information necessary to host and attend the event.

An in-person event media kit should include:
- Event Poster
- Event Flyer
- Admission Cost
- Admission Requirements
- Location
- Hours
- Event Details
- Contact Info
- Book Cover
- Book Description
- Release Date
- Author Photo
- Author Bio
- Social Media Links

In addition to the author and book information provided in a media kit for a virtual event, in-person events require event details such as the location, hours, and admission cost, requirements, and restrictions. If an event is 18+, for example, make sure that detail is listed clearly in the media kit.

Posters and flyers that are eye-catching and provide the event details are important for events like book signings and book release parties. Some venues create their own posters or have their own print advertising requirements. Check with the venue before going to the expense of creating your own, and make sure you have their permission before using their logo.

Having the author information, book information, and event details in the event media kit will help with the event planning and promotion. If you make the experience easy and enjoyable, it's more likely that a venue will ask you to return for future events.

PRO TIP: Check that poster images are high resolution (300 dpi) for printing and all materials have been proofread for errors. I also recommend providing images in sizes optimized for both print and the web. This way your flyers can be handed out, posters printed and hung, and the promotional images can be added to the venue's event page. Make it easy for people to promote your event.

CHAPTER 6:
CREATING A MARKETING PLAN

    Your marketing plan outlines your advertising and marketing efforts for the upcoming year. A marketing plan will help you set goals, demonstrate your goals to others, create strategies, and stay within your budget. Using a marketing plan will also help with time management, so that you can set aside time for book promotion and time for writing.

    Strengths and Weaknesses:
    Begin by assessing your marketing strengths, weaknesses, opportunities, and threats. Brainstorm what comes to mind, then dig deeper with research. I like to keep up on market trends, new technology, and emerging opportunities like new book and fantasy conventions throughout the year. I add to my brainstorming file as new information becomes available, making it easier to create next year's plan, and, if the information is of a significant enough change, I update my current marketing plan when necessary.
    Here's an example of initial brainstorming:
    Strengths (strong author platform: Twitter, Facebook, Blog)
    Weaknesses (no public speaking experience, no control over book price)
    Opportunities (growing audio market, new local events, new local book store, book tie-in with holidays or events)
    Threats (downturn in economy, change in consumer habits, new technology, the unknown, increase in competition for book sales and for book ads)
    When assessing your strengths and weaknesses, consider how much control you have over your books. If traditionally published, you may not have control over your book's pricing. Unless you can get your publisher to agree to coordinate with your marketing efforts, you may not be able to

run a limited time price promotion. Make a list of questions to ask your agent and/or publisher. If self-published, consider limitations such as distribution limitations from using Kindle Unlimited or royalty share contract restrictions.

Target Audience:
Identify your target audience. Your target audience will include the target readers you identified when creating your author platform. Consider your reader's demographics (age, gender, location, and language), reading habits (genre, series or stand alone, novel or short fiction, ebooks and/or physical books and/or audiobooks), shopping habits (bargain shopper, new release shopper, library or brick-and-mortar stores or online retailers) and where they hang out (Twitter, Facebook, specific blogs).

I find it increasingly helpful to keep and organize information regarding target audience in annual charts and graphs. Pie charts are a great visual way to look at reader demographics, reading habits, and shopping habits. Make charts annually (or quarterly) to look at shifts in your target audience over time. There are many reasons for these shifts, some of your doing (change in genre, release schedule) and some outside your control (market trends, new technology). Being aware of changes over time will help you refine your goals and strategies.

Marketing Goals:
List your marketing goals. I find it's easiest to start by jotting down general goals first and gradually work toward more specific objectives. An outline format with headings and subheadings works well for organizing your list in this way.

For example, start with a goal to sell more books, define a specific percentage of overall increase in book sales, and set a specific goal for number of books sold per day, month, and/or year by format.

If you're just starting out marketing your first book, you may not have a lot of sales and marketing data to go by. List your general marketing goals now and come back to refine those goals throughout the year as you gain data and experience. It's better to have general goals than none at all.

Budget:
Set your marketing budget based on how much money you have available to spend on marketing. Consider your royalty income, other income, and amount spent on marketing in recent years.

Marketing Strategies:
List the marketing strategies and tactics you plan to use throughout the year. You'll find many strategies within the pages of this book. There's even a handy checklist in the back.

Once you decide which strategies to use, put your list into a spreadsheet. Add a column for price of each tactic. Use the sum feature on your spreadsheet to total the price column to make sure you don't go over your budget.

You will want to spread some of your marketing throughout the year, while some will be concentrated around the time of specific events such as a book release or holidays. Make sure to consider time-related restrictions on any particular marketing method.

A digital calendar is a great tool for planning out your annual marketing. Once you set your dates, add a date column to your spreadsheet. To view your marketing strategies chronologically, you can sort the spreadsheet by descending or ascending date using the date column. You can also add a column to specify type of marketing, giving the ability to sort by type (such as online ads, offline ads, sell sheet/postcard mailings, blog/virtual tours, giveaways, public appearances, and price promotions), and use a color coding system for color filling each row.

PRO TIP: Set realistic goals and a conservative marketing budget. Not all books make a profit and not all marketing strategies work. If you do earn more than expected on a new book release, set some of that "bonus" royalty money aside to increase your marketing budget while there is already buying momentum.

CHAPTER 7: BOOK SWAG AND PROMOTIONAL ITEMS

You know that free pen you got from your doctor's office, the stress ball your yoga instructor gave out, or the free calendar you receive in the mail each year from your heating company? Those companies, small business owners, and medical professionals gave away free, custom, personalized promotional items to help promote their business and increase customer loyalty.

Giving away free promotional items is smart business. Promotional items (swag) can promote your book, your author brand, and create customer loyalty. In order to make swag a part of your book marketing strategy, you need to make a plan for designing, creating, and distributing your promotional items.

Keep your marketing budget in mind when selecting promotional items. Book swag comes in two basic types, paper (sometimes referred to as print swag) and premium. Paper swag is less expensive and easier to ship, especially when mailing outside the country. In an effort to reduce waste, some conventions will not accept paper swag in welcome bags for attendees. Some blogs will only host giveaways for prizes over a certain dollar value. Premium swag is more expensive, but is better suited as giveaway prizes.

Top Paper Book Swag:
- Business Cards
- Book flats
- Bookmarks
- Book Plates
- Maps
- Postcards

- Posters
- Stickers
- Temporary Tattoos
- Trading Cards

Top Premium Book Swag:
- Bags (Tote Bags, Drawstring Bags)
- Book Charms
- Buttons
- Candles
- Candy
- Coffee Mugs
- Drink Koozies
- Eyeglass Cloths
- Flashlights
- Jewelry
- Keychains
- Lip Balm
- Notepads
- Pens
- T-shirts
- Travel Mugs
- Water Bottles

What to Choose:

Not all swag is created equal, but it can be tailored to you, your brand, and your books. Do your books take place in a small coffee shop? Perhaps cup cozies or coffee mugs would be perfect. What if your brand is about romance? What if you had heart shaped boxes with your logo and website inside? Some swag is more desirable to the swag collectors, but standing out by spending too much money is never a good idea. If you can tailor swag to your brand, the reader will be able to more closely associate you to the swag they enjoy when they get home.

Design:

Make sure your author name and website are on the item. Other great things to include are your logo, tagline, and book cover. QR codes directing visitors to a landing site are a helpful addition to postcards.

Items will need to look professional and the design for each item should optimize the product dimensions and materials. Match item colors to your author brand or book cover, and use text colors that contrast with the background color. Avoid blurry products by uploading only high-resolution images.

Printing sites should have the image specifications available and often provide downloadable templates. You can also hire a designer to do the work for you.

Create:

Decide if you are custom printing directly on the item or making custom printed stickers to add to items. Whether purchasing custom items, or custom stickers and items to add the stickers to, most companies offer quantity discounts. Try to create promotional items that you can use for more than one event. You can order more and take advantage of the quantity discounts if the item is suited for giveaways, raffles, mailing list rewards, and welcome bags.

There are many sites that offer custom printing. The sites below are popular.

Custom Printing Sites:
- GotPrint
- National Pen
- Print Runner
- VistaPrint

Custom Label/Sticker Sites:
- Evermine
- Lightning Labels
- StickerYou
- TinyPrints
- VistaPrint

You can also find custom printed items and labels on Etsy.

PRO TIP: Shop for bargains and sign up for email alerts with sales and coupon codes. My favorite way to stay current on the most up-to-date sales and coupon codes is by using Ebates (ebates.com).

Distribute:

You can offer promotional items for free to entice shoppers to your vendor table, to sign up for your mailing list, or come out for your book signing. Use as gift items to reward fan club members, beta readers, and newsletter subscribers. Promotional items also make great giveaway prizes and raffle items.

Conventions and events give away welcome bags to registered attendees. Those welcome bags are often stuffed with swag and free books. Make sure to check with event staff months prior to the event to see what types of swag they accept (many will not accept paper swag), who they will accept items from (some will only accept from attending authors or sponsor publishers), and if there is a bag stuffing fee. Offer to send swag to events that are outside your price range or geographic area to expand your reach and have an author presence from the comfort of your home, or provide swag for an event you are attending to build customer loyalty with attendees.

If selling books at signings and conventions or on your website, use premium swag as a bonus item for sales over a certain quantity or dollar amount to encourage readers to buy more books. Custom tote bags are a great item to offer to readers who purchase more than three books. Tote bags make it easier for shoppers to buy and carry more items, and they'll be advertising your author brand wherever they go.

CHAPTER 8: BLOG TOURS, COVER REVEALS, AND BOOK BLASTS

Blog Tours, cover reveals, and book blasts are virtual tours that you can do from the comfort of your own home. Online tours do take planning, but they are much more cost-effective than going on a real life, in-person tour with travel, lodging, and convention expenses.

The first thing you need to decide is if you are going to run the tour or hire a blog tour company to run the event for you. You can run your own blog tour (tips in the HOW TO section below) or hire a PR or blog tour company.

Popular PR firms and virtual blog tour companies include:
- Bewitching Book Tours
- Enchanted Book Promotions
- Goddess Fish Promotions
- InkSlinger PR
- Pump Up Your Book
- PureTextuality PR
- Reading Addiction Virtual Book Tours
- Rockstar Book Tours
- Xpresso Book Tours
- YA Bound Book Tours

If you hire a PR or tour company, find out exactly what services are included. Many companies will create the signup form and event headers and buttons, make a landing page for sign ups, email their blogger list and share on social media, keep track of sign ups, put together the event media kit, and send all tour materials to each participating blogger. Read the company's details to make sure that all of these services are included in the package you are purchasing. Also, be clear on the number of participating bloggers, and if the number of participants is guaranteed.

PRO TIP: Look at the PR or tour company's current blog tours. You are paying for their blog contacts, so make sure that those blogs are high quality blogs with great engagement rates.

Do they look professional? Are the event headers and buttons eye-catching? Is there evidence of reader engagement (comments, likes, shares, giveaway entries)? Are the participating blogs quality blogs with good blog design, working comment forms, and a large number of followers? Do they share their posts to active social media sites? Do they blog frequently?

Once you decide who is running the tour, you need to set a tour date. Ideally, the date will coincide with your book release or cover reveal day.

Give bloggers and tour companies as much lead time as possible. Bloggers are busy and often schedule their posts in advance. As a blogger myself, I schedule my blog posts up to 60-90 days in advance. If an author comes to me with a last minute request, I am often already too booked and too busy to help them.

Consider that bloggers are volunteers who work for free. Be considerate of their time and their schedule. Also, blog posts take time to write and format. Do not inconvenience bloggers with belated, unreasonable requests.

PRO TIP: A great time saving tool for bloggers is being provided the HTML for a promo post. If you use Blogger or Wordpress, create the blog post ahead of time. If you click on HTML, you'll see the HTML for the post. Select all, copy, and paste into a text file for sharing with bloggers. Remember to provide all tour information, images, guest post, and giveaway form embed codes separately so that bloggers can customize their individual blog posts. Let bloggers know at sign up that easy copy-and-paste blog post HTML will be made available. This information will encourage participation from bloggers who are busy and don't have time to fully write and format your promo post from scratch.

Your tour planning will depend on the type of tour. The most common types of blog tours are:
- Cover Reveal
- Release Tour
- Book Blitz
- Review Tour

Cover Reveal:
Cover reveal tours are for revealing your cover art to the world at an exact time across all media sites. Do not post or share your book cover anywhere prior to your set cover reveal time. You can tease with sneak peeks, so long as the entire cover is not revealed.
A cover reveal event helps to create buzz before a book's release. Include the book cover, book description, formats, publisher, release date, author bio, author website, social media links, and, if available, a link to the book's preorder page. Most cover reveal events also feature a giveaway and some include a book excerpt, author guest post, or interview.

Release Tour:
Release tours take place on or just after the book's release day. In addition to the information above, release tours provide all purchase links. Release tours should provide each blogger with a book excerpt, author guest post, author interview, character interview, book or series playlist, or a top ten list related to the new book release. These tours usually last one to four weeks with stops at one to three blogs each day.

Book Blitz:
A book blitz is a fast and furious tour, often on a book's release day or release anniversary, typically lasting one to four days. Blog post materials are less unique, often including the book and author info, a book excerpt, and a giveaway.

Review Tour:
A review tour requires that each participating blogger read a review copy of your book and post their review within

the dates of the tour. Bloggers are provided with the book and author information. They are also given review copies, or ARCs if prior to the book release, in exchange for an honest review. Reviewers cannot be paid and their opinions cannot be influenced. The review must be honest, and there is no guarantee that a review will be posted. Sometimes during review tours bloggers will refrain from posting a negative review until after the tour is over, but this is a courtesy and cannot be forced.

PRO TIP: Don't burn bridges, but do extend an olive branch. If a reviewer contacts you to say that they did not like the book and will not be posting a review on the agreed upon date, ask if they'd like you to provide a guest post. This helps out the blogger and builds a positive relationship. They may not have liked this one book, but they might become a fan of your other work.

HOW TO: Running your own blog tour takes a lot of time and effort. It also requires having a list of contacts or a willingness to send out to cold contacts. Check voluntary blog listing sites like the Book Blogger Directory (bookbloggerdirectory.wordpress.com), The Book Blogger List (bookbloggerlist.com), Indie Book Reviewer (indiebookreviewer.wordpress.com), Blog Nation (blognation.com), KidLitosphere Bloggers (kidlitosphere.org/bloggers/), or the YA Book Blog Directory (yabookblogdirectory.blogspot.com) for blogs in your genre.

Never buy contact lists and never contact bloggers without first reading their policy page. A blogger's policy page will give you insight into target age, publishing status (self-published or trade published), and genre restrictions, and if the blogger is accepting requests for reviews, tours, guest posts, interviews, or to host giveaways.

PRO TIP: Never add an attachment to an email when sending out cold contacts. Most bloggers will not open an email with a paperclip from an unknown source. If you want to add a book cover or author photo in your query email, use a link to the photo instead of an attachment.

When reaching out to bloggers, be polite (you are asking them for a favor), address them by their first name (usually found on their About Me page, blog sidebar, or at the bottom of their blog posts), spell their name and blog name correctly, and state clearly who you are, what you write, and what you want. Having a professional email address and informative email signature with links back to your website and blog will help.

If the blogger has a format for requests, such as using a required tagline and providing specific information, methodically follow the instructions. This may require using a contact form instead of emailing them directly. Do what they ask.

Bloggers don't create policy rules lightly. Policies are complicated and boring to write, so if they took the time to write a policy, they expect authors to stick to it. Contact forms and required taglines can save bloggers hours of sifting through requests from authors who never bothered to read the policy page. The authors who follow the rules will get past the slush pile.

Make it clear how to sign up for the tour. Should the blogger respond by email or is there a signup form to fill out?

I highly recommend creating a signup form. I use Google Docs Forms, found in Google Drive, for my blog tour signup form. The forms are easy to make and all data gathered is exported into a spreadsheet.

PRO TIP: Go into the spreadsheet for your Google Docs signup form, click on the **Tools** tab, and click on **Notification Rules**. Select how often you wish to be notified of changes to your form. If you set your notification settings to email you whenever a blogger signs up, you can immediately contact them with a thank you message and the media kit and any other materials they need for the tour.

When creating a signup form, designate the mandatory fields. I require that visitors fill out their name, email address, blog name, and blog address (URL). I make these required fields text fields. Use checkbox style fields for questions asking bloggers to make a selection of what parts of a tour they want to participate in. Add a text or paragraph field where visitors can leave any additional questions or comments.

Once you've created your form, include a direct link to the signup form in query emails to bloggers and post it on social networks. When sharing to Twitter, you can add the hashtags #blog, #bloggers, and #bloggerswanted to your tweet. There are Facebook groups dedicated to sharing blog tour sign up information. If you're posting to a group or forum, check the posting rules and make sure to follow the rules and that the book you are touring matches the genre of the bloggers you're soliciting.

You will need to put together a media kit for your tour. A professional looking tour header and/or button featuring the tour dates and book cover are helpful. Include the book cover, book description, available formats, publisher, release date, author bio, author photos, author website, social media links, and purchase links. If you've received a review quote from a major celebrity, add that to the media kit. Including optional HTML code for the blog post is also helpful and may increase the percentage of bloggers who post your tour post on time.

Depending on the type of tour, you might also need to include a giveaway, interview, guest post, and/or review copy of your book. More information on giveaways, interviews and guest posts, and book reviews and ARC reviews in the next three chapters.

Try to send the media kit and any other tour materials two to three weeks before the tour begins. Any earlier (with the exception of any bloggers who request they receive materials early) and bloggers might forget about your post. Any later and bloggers won't have time to create and schedule your post. If you are careful not to sound rude or pushy, you can send a friendly reminder email to participating bloggers 48 hours before the tour begins. Let them know that you are available if they have any questions or concerns.

CHAPTER 9:
GIVEAWAYS

Giveaways can help you gain exposure, increase social media followers, get reviews, and get your book added to reader's TBR (To Be Read) lists. Giving away prizes can also help to build brand loyalty by giving winners, and their friends and family, a sense of good will toward you for giving them something for free.

If you use promotional items that are tied to your author brand and feature your name, website, and/or book cover, those giveaway prizes will continue marketing for you. Every time a bookmark or tote bag is used and a t-shirt or button is worn, new people will be exposed to your author brand. If the person showing off the product is one of your readers, there's a good chance that their friends will also be part of your target audience, making this organic exposure a form of target marketing.

When planning a giveaway, you'll need to consider the what, where, how, and why. In other words, you need to decide what the prize will be, where your giveaway will take place, how readers will enter, and why you are having the giveaway.

What:

The three most popular types of giveaways are book giveaways, gift card giveaways, and swag giveaways. The purpose of giving away books is to gain more reviews. Gift cards are usually to book retailers like Amazon or Barnes & Noble, and the hope is that the winner will purchase your book, giving its ranking a boost. Swag giveaways are for promotional items and help expand reach and establish your author brand.

Sometimes authors will give away the chance to have the winner's name included in one of their stories. Less common are giveaways to take a limited number of winners out with the author. This often is over coffee or dinner with the author, but you can get creative.

PRO TIP: If taking readers out as part of a giveaway prize, try to tie the event or event location to your books. When I was in Atlanta for a book signing, I held a giveaway to take a group of readers on a tour of Oakland Cemetery followed by appetizers across the street at Six Feet Under Pub. I've also brought readers on ghost tours. The cemetery tours, ghost tours, and cemetery-themed pub tie in with the paranormal books that I write.

It also helps to schedule these special reader meet-ups just prior to a book signing. After the event, give the winners custom tote bags filled with swag and tell them if they'd like anything signed, then come see you at the book signing.

Decide on the type of prize and the number of winners. Keep in mind shipping fees for physical items, especially if offering to ship to international destinations. If sending physical prizes, you may want to limit the number of winners so that you don't go over your book marketing budget.

PRO TIP: If shipping books and paper swag domestically, you can send your prizes out at "book rate" with the United States Postal Service. The package may take a little longer to reach its destination, but it will cost you significantly less than using priority mail.

You also must decide where you are willing to ship prizes. Sending international mail is costly, especially when trying to ship packages to countries other than Canada or the United Kingdom, but might be worth it if you're trying to expand your reach in foreign book markets. If the giveaway is part of a blog tour, more bloggers will sign up to host a giveaway that's open to mailing addresses worldwide. This is especially true of bloggers who reside outside the United States. You can make your giveaway open to the US, US/CA/UK, or make it international.

One way to avoid shipping costs is to offer a digital prize. You can offer an ebook, an audiobook digital download, or digital gift card. Ebooks can be sent as an email attachment, by sending the winner a Smashwords coupon code, or by using a book distribution service like BookFunnel.

Another way to avoid shipping costs is offer an item that is available through a retailer that offers free worldwide shipping. My favorite is The Book Depository. They have over 9 million titles, offer free shipping to over 100 countries with no minimum order, and if you use Ebates when you order, you'll get 2.5% cash back.

If you send a digital prize or a book through The Book Depository, consider sending a signed postcard or bookplate to the winner. Signed swag is always highly sought after, adds a personal touch, and a postcard or bookplate can feature your author name and website. You can purchase international stamps from any post office. If your winner is from the US, remember that domestic postcard stamps are cheaper than letter stamps. If buying either type, get the forever stamps so you don't get stuck needing to add additional postage when the post office changes stamp prices.

Where:

There are many places to hold a giveaway, including on your website and social media sites, on blog tour participating blogs, on a Facebook page or event page, Amazon giveaways, Goodreads FirstReads giveaways, LibraryThing monthly giveaways, or in person at an event.

Where you hold your giveaway is directly related to how readers can enter and why you're having the giveaway. When giveaways are held online, it's easy to use electronic entry forms or allow for comment entry. In-person giveaways allow for entry through interactions such as dice games and other games of chance.

Online giveaways are the best way to grow your social media following and get your book added to TBR lists on sites like Goodreads or LibraryThing. Newsletter subscribers can be added through both online and in-person giveaways, but you'll gain a larger percentage of new subscribers with online giveaways, especially those that use an electronic entry form.

The primary reason for in-person giveaways is to increase traffic to your signing table or vendor table. Not only will the chance to win prizes attract readers to your table, but having those people in front of your table will give the appearance of popularity. Other attendees will see a happy crowd at your table and wonder what is so fun and interesting, drawing even more people over to your table.

PRO TIP: An empty table and a blank signup sheet are uninviting. Ask a friend or an assistant to come to your table and "seed the pot" by signing up for your mailing list and playing one of your games of chance. You can even take turns doing this with other authors to help each other out. When attendees see that something is happening at your table, they'll come to investigate.

How:
Giveaway entry methods vary depending on where the giveaway takes place. The most popular methods of entry for online giveaways are by electronic form or comments (blog, Facebook, Twitter). The most popular method of entry for in-person giveaways are games of chance.

The best giveaway entry method for online giveaways is electronic form. Rafflecopter (rafflecopter.com), Gleam (gleam.io), and Woorise (woorise.com) all offer customizable, embeddable forms, collect data, and provide useful analytics.

Each form tool offers a range of pricing depending on what features you need. Rafflecopter has packages for $0, $13, $43, and $84 per month. Gleam has packages for $0, $39, and $149 per month. Woorise has packages for $29, $49, $99, and $199 per month. Forms become more customizable and offer more author branding as the package price increases.

My preferred giveaway form tool is Rafflecopter. It offers a free option or you can upgrade to a paid service for additional features. This makes it a great risk-free tool if you're uncertain if you need an expensive form tool.

Rafflecopter forms are easy to create and share. Click on **New Giveaway** to create a new giveaway. If you've used Rafflecopter before, you can click **Duplicate a Giveaway** in the right sidebar to clone any previous giveaway form with its entry options. If starting from scratch, click the **Add a Prize** button and type in your prize.

Be concise. If you're offering a huge prize pack filled with dragon themed books and swag, it's better to say Dragon Prize Pack here on the form, and list all the items in the prize pack in the giveaway post on your blog or Facebook.

Once you type in a prize, the giveaway **Nickname** field will appear in the right sidebar and will autofill with the name of your prize. You can change the name of the giveaway without changing the prize listed on the form.

A **Terms & Conditions** field will appear below the Nickname field. You can click **Pre-fill with our Easy Template** or write your own from scratch.

Scroll down to **People Can Enter By** and click **Add an Entry Option** to begin adding ways for readers to enter. Try to keep to five or less entry options. More than five entry options will overwhelm many potential fans. Select the type of entry option you want. Some options are for paid subscribers only, but following a Twitter account, commenting on a blog post, and the invent your own option are free.

When you're done adding entry options, provide the giveaway **Start Date** and **End Date**. I highly recommend setting your start date one day early and your end date one day late to allow for readers in different time zones.

Click the **Preview & Install** button to move to the **Installation** tab where you can look over and approve your form. If you need to change anything, just go back to the **Setup** page. In fact, you can log in and make changes to your form at any time, even while your giveaway is running. All changes happen in real-time on all forms on every website.

To share your giveaway form, you can provide a link to the form or embed the form on websites. Rafflecopter provides easy copy-and-paste embed code. From the **Installation** tab, in the **Embed in a Blog or Website** section, click the **Copy** button to copy your form's embed code.

If the giveaway is part of a blog tour, include the form link and embed code in the media kit for participating bloggers. To embed in a blog or website post, go to the HTML tab of your blog or website's post dashboard and paste the form where you want it in the post.

If you embed the form in a blog post before the giveaway begins, the form will state that the giveaway has not yet begun. During the giveaway timeframe, the form will give a countdown of the number of days and hours left to enter, creating a sense of urgency. When a giveaway is over, the form will state that the giveaway is over and the form is no longer accepting entries.

PRO TIP: Do not try to embed your giveaway form in your email newsletter. The javascript will likely be disabled and might be flagged as malicious code. Instead, run the giveaway on your website or blog, and in your newsletter provide a link to where the giveaway is taking place.

Why:
The most basic reason to give something away is to sell more books. Giveaways can do this by getting your book cover, description, excerpts, and buy links out in front of readers and by having readers add your book to their TBR lists. Giveaways also build a sense of good will and increase brand loyalty. Indirectly, but just as importantly, giveaways have the ability to expand your social media reach by gaining new followers, increasing engagement. You can also grow your target marketing by getting new mailing list and/or newsletter subscribers.

Once you decide on a specific reason for having a giveaway, make the thing you want to increase one of your entry options. Sites like Rafflecopter will allow you to allot points that give more weight to an entry method you want to focus on.

For example, if you want more Twitter followers, make following you on Twitter one of the entry options.

Creating targeted entry options is easy if using a Rafflecopter giveaway form. Also, by narrowing down your marketing goals for the giveaway, you can more easily reduce the number of giveaway entry options. Surveys show that readers prefer giveaways with one to five entry options. This keeps the rules simple and easy to follow and makes entry less time-consuming.

PRO TIP: Share your giveaway on all of your social media sites, website, blog, and newsletter. Submit a link to your giveaway to giveaway listing sites and giveaway Facebook groups for even greater reach. Not only will you get more entries, but you'll be spreading the word about your book and author brand.

CHAPTER 10: INTERVIEWS AND GUEST POSTS

Interviews and guest posts allow readers to get to know you. They're also a great way to expand your reach to the audience of blogs, magazines, newspapers, podcasts, vlogs and booktube channels, television stations, and radio. While you have the attention of this new, larger audience take the opportunity to shine.

Do share:
- Book Info
- Author Info
- Writing Process
- Hobbies
- Pets*

Use caution when sharing:
- Personal Info
- Real Name
- School Names
- Child Names
- Pet Names

Use your interview or guest post to talk about your books. Give readers a glimpse behind the curtain. Talk about what inspired a character, book, or series. Explain your writing, research, plotting, and/or world building process. Share funny stories related to your writing and publishing journey.

Let the audience get to know you. Do you have any hobbies or pets? Do you have special knowledge or credentials that helped in writing your books? Stick to topics that can relate back to your books and that do not contradict your author brand.

I recommend not letting an interview or guest post get too personal. It's fine to ask about your writing habits, reading habits, and your favorite book, movie, or food. It's not, in my opinion, okay to be asked for your real name (if you write under a pen name), age, relationship status, sales numbers, or royalty earnings.

Imagine walking up to a stranger at a coffee shop. What would you be willing to share with them?

PRO TIP: Being an author rock star can be fun, but being a celebrity comes with risks. Use caution when sharing information in an interview or guest post. Ask yourself how revealing a piece of information to the public might harm your author brand or make you vulnerable to security threats and identity theft.

Provide your author media kit as soon as you're invited to participate in an interview or guest post. This will give your press contact a chance to read up on you, helping to encourage a better introduction and quality interview questions. Your media kit will also make it easier to add your relevant, up-to-date author bio, photo, book cover, and social media links to any posts or online calendar listings.

CHAPTER 11: BOOK REVIEWS AND ARC REVIEWS

Authors need book reviews. Book reviews are more likely to persuade a reader's purchase decision than hard-sell advertising and promotions.

Your book's reviews will impact all aspects of your book marketing plan. The number of reviews, average star rating, quality of reviews, and additional editorial reviews will influence sales, impact your ability to get blogger event sign ups and get invited to speak on panels in your book's genre, and receive approval from top tier promotional sites like BookBub, Ereader News Today, and Free Booksy (more on promotional sites in **Chapter 14: Advertising and Price Promotions**). Reviews posted to non-retail sites, like book social media sites (Goodreads, Shelfari, BookLikes, LibraryThing) and book blogs, are organic marketing that can create buzz before, during, and long after a book's release.

PRO TIP: Positive reviews are wonderful, but even negative book reviews can get readers looking at and talking about your book. Sometimes what one reader dislikes will appeal to another reader and that negative review will have gained you a new sale and possibly a new fan.

Reviews organically amplify awareness of your book and boost sales. But just because the outcome is organic, you can't sit back and expect to gain reviews without doing any work. Create a book review campaign as part of your marketing strategy.

In this chapter, we'll cover how to create and run a successful book review campaign that will get you reviews before, during, and after release.

ARC Reviews:

ARCs are a smart marketing strategy geared at garnering early reviews. Provide ebook ARCs and print book ARCs to reviewers two to six months before your book's release day. Encourage early reviewers to share their reviews to blogs and social media to create buzz for your book before its release. Early buzz can lead to pre-order sales and release day sales.

On release day, send out a friendly reminder to reviewers that reviews posted to your book's retail pages are highly appreciated. Include direct links to your book's retail product pages and a link to your author media kit and your book's media kit.

Finding Reviewers:
Begin any search for book reviewers by identifying the type of book in need of review. What is the book's target age group? What is the book's genre and subgenre? Is the book self-published or traditionally published? What formats are you promoting? Is the book a new or upcoming release?

Most book reviewers have very strict policies on what books they are willing to review, or if they are even accepting unsolicited books at the moment. Narrow your search to reviewers with a reputation for reviewing in your genre. Once you find the reviewer, read their review policy.

If your book is a good fit for the reviewer and is not disqualified by their review policy, contact the reviewer using the provided email or contact form. Follow any submission rules in the review policy for email subject line, information to provide, and the order and format in which to provide it.

PRO TIP: Unless the review policy specifically asks for something to be provided as an attachment, do not add an attachment of any kind to your initial query message. Most unsolicited emails with attachments get deleted or sent to the spam folder without ever being read.

Be polite in all correspondence with reviewers, use a clear subject line heading, and address messages to the reviewer by name. Do not send out a mass email. Mass emails are rude and impersonal and may end up flagged as spam. If you do not have the time to send out individual, personalized messages, then hire a PR company, personal assistant, review service, or blog review tour company to do it for you.

PRO TIP: If you hire someone to contact reviewers on your behalf, ask to see the letter they intend to mail before they send it. Grammar and spelling mistakes, formatting errors, rudeness, or incorrect information will reflect poorly on you and your author brand.

Most review services have their own list of contacts and participating bloggers. When you hire a review service, ask how large their contact list is, how many people they plan to contact on your behalf, and if the cost of their services comes with a guaranteed minimum number of sign ups.

If cold contacting reviewers yourself, whether as your only strategy or to supplement beyond a review service's list of contacts, you will need to create your own contact list. You can search for reviewers in genre appropriate Facebook groups, Goodreads groups, LibraryThing groups, forums, and blogger directories. Although time consuming, I also recommend doing a search engine search for book blogs in your genre.

Check voluntary blog listing sites like the Book Blogger Directory (bookbloggerdirectory.wordpress.com), The Book Blogger List (bookbloggerlist.com), Indie Book Reviewer (indiebookreviewer.wordpress.com), Blog Nation (blognation.com), KidLitosphere Bloggers (kidlitosphere.org/bloggers/), Book Reviewer Yellow Pages (bookrevieweryellowpages.com), or the YA Book Blog Directory (yabookblogdirectory.blogspot.com) for blogs in your genre.

Giveaways are also an effective way to get books and ARCs into the hands of interested readers who might post a review. Read **Chapter 9: Giveaways** on how to make giveaways a part of your book review campaign.

Distributing Books for Review:
If you're sending books out or you've hired a PR or blog tour company to send out review copies, there are four easy ways to send ebooks to reviewers—an ebook distribution service like Bookfunnel, Smashwords coupon code, email attachment, or cloud sharing link.

Give your reviewers options, not limitations. Offer multiple ebook formats, such as mobi, epub, and pdf. If using Smashwords, make sure that all formats are checked off in the book's settings. Reviewers do not have every type of reading device, so offering only one format will reduce the number of reviewers who can participate.

Bookfunnel (bookfunnel.com) is a paid service that gets books to readers and provides customer support to field any questions or problems along the way. Bookfunnel subscription plans range in price from $20, $100, and $200 per year for individual authors.

NetGalley (www.netgalley.com) is another great way to get ebooks and eARCs in the hands of reviewers, but, while their pricing for individual authors has come down in recent years, their service is expensive (around $399 to list a title for six months). If you are looking to save money, consider joining a professional organization that offers a reduced group rate for NetGalley. SFWA offers a reduced rate on approved science fiction or fantasy books from active members, and Broad Universe offers a reduced rate (around $30 for one month) on approved speculative fiction books by active members. This NetGalley savings alone can offset your membership dues, and you'll avoid the more lengthy NetGalley registration process required for individual authors and small publishers.

After Review:

If you ran a successful book review campaign, your book received new reviews. There are a few things that you can do to boost the signal on positive reviews. These strategies are not mandatory, but they are smart marketing. You can:
- Boost Amazon Review
- Like/Share Social Media Posts
- Like/Share Review Blog Posts
- Quote Reviews

On Amazon, you can give well-written, positive reviews a boost. Go to your book's Amazon product page and click on **Customer Reviews** located below the title and author name. You will jump to the **Customer Reviews** section at the bottom of the page. Click the **Number** beside the gold stars to be taken to the dedicated **Customer Reviews** page for your book. You will see the **Top Positive Review** and **Top Critical Review**. One of the factors that makes these "top" reviews is the number of helpful votes they have received. Voting that a review is helpful will give your book and the review a boost. Scroll down to find reviews. There are options for filtering your results. At the bottom of each review there are two buttons. When you find a good review, click the **Yes** button to give Amazon feedback that this is a helpful review.

If a review is particularly nasty (threatens you, your editor, or cover designer as an individual), you can click the **No** button, but use the No button sparingly. Do not abuse the No button.

You can also give participating blogger's a boost on social media. Most bloggers will share their reviews and links to their review posts on their social media sites. Liking and sharing those social media posts will drive traffic to their blog and their review. This gets more people to see the review and increases click-through rate of retailer links in the post which drives sales. You'll be doing the blogger a favor and helping your book's organic marketing.

Boosting the blogger's blog post will have a similar effect. Use the social share buttons at the bottom of the blog post to share the post to your social media sites. You can also pin the book cover in the post to a Pinterest board, and click the like, star, or heart button at the bottom of the post to show that the post was enjoyable.

Editorial reviews, including reviews from highly reputable book blogs, can be added to your book's product pages, book cover, your website, and your book media kit or author media kit. Editorial reviews should be direct quotes from reliable, professional review sources and must be short in length. Remember to include the review source with the review quote.

PRO TIP: Some retailers, like NOOK Press, provide a field for adding editorial reviews during the publishing process. Other retailers, like Amazon, provide an option for adding editorial reviews once the book's product page has been published. We'll cover how to use Amazon's Author Central to add editorial reviews to Amazon product pages in the next chapter, **Chapter 12: Retail Product Pages**.

In addition to the review itself, you may receive correspondence from reviewers. If a reviewer messages you that they loved your book and posted a review, reply with a thank you. If a reviewer messages you that they hated your book and posted a review, reply with a thank you or do not reply at all.

If you provide a free book to the reviewer, it is in exchange for an HONEST review. There is no obligation for a review to be positive. That is why reviews are so influential.

PRO TIP: NEVER respond to negative reviews. NEVER contact a reviewer about a negative review. NEVER threaten, harass, or argue with reviewers.

CHAPTER 12: RETAIL PRODUCT PAGES

Retail product pages are the gateway to your books. The product page is the landing page featuring your book's cover image, description, reviews, and purchase options. Some product pages also provide an author bio and link to more of your books. Knowing how to create and update your product pages is vital to your book's success.

There are many product page pitfalls to avoid, including low quality cover images, grammar mistakes, incorrect or inadequate keywords, and poor formatting. In this chapter, we'll cover the common pitfalls to avoid and easy ways to improve the look and effectiveness of your retail product pages.

DO:
- Quality Book Cover Image
- Include Book Awards
- NYT & USA Today Bestseller
- Enticing Blurb/Description
- Professionally Edit Blurb and Bio
- Quality Author Photo
- Up-To-Date Author Bio
- Editorial Reviews
- Quality Keywords
- Accurate Categories
- Link Print, Ebook, and Audio
- Update and Make Corrections

DO NOT:
- Low Quality Book Cover
- Long Titles
- Title in ALL CAPS
- Mentioning Format in Title
- Spelling Mistakes

- Grammar Mistakes
- Review Quotes in Blurb
- Sale Info in Blurb
- Address/Phone Number
- Review Quotes in Blurb
- False Claims
- Incorrect Series Numbering
- Formatting Mistakes

Release day can be hectic. I highly recommend having your book cover, description, and author bio prepared in advance. It is also helpful to plan your keywords and know your book's categories before publishing your book. Check out the helpful tips below before publishing. Thankfully, if you learn something new in this chapter, you can make changes to books that are already published. Read this chapter's HOW TO for information on how to use Amazon's Author Central, one of the most powerful tools indie authors have for maintaining their book's Amazon product pages. Author Central can help you control product page content and formatting at any time.

BOOK COVER: Your book's cover art must be a high quality design and fit your book's genre. In addition to uploading an eye-catching cover, make sure that the file you upload is in high resolution. Low-resolution images will look blurry and will reflect poorly on the overall quality of your book.

SAMPLING: Most retailers will allow readers to read a sample of your book. If you're using a company like Smashwords to distribute to retailers, you will need to select the sampling percentage. The sampling percentage is the percentage of the book that readers can read for free and is calculated from the book's first page. Most authors choose 15-20%. Some retailers will choose their own sampling percentage, usually letting readers read 5-20% for free.

Amazon has its own sampling program, Look Inside. If your Kindle book is published through KPD, your book is automatically enrolled in Look Inside. Adding the Look Inside feature to print books requires publisher enrollment.

Publishers must sign up for this program, agree to Amazon's terms, and certify that they are the rights holder.

TITLE: Do not enter your title in ALL CAPS. Most retailers have restrictions against this practice and will not publish your book if the title is in ALL CAPS. Do not include trademarks, reference other authors, or make claims like "free" or "bestseller" in your book's title.

Lengthy titles are also to be avoided. Studies have shown that readers tend to skim past titles with over 60 characters. Good SEO practice is to keep titles under 50 characters. Words with difficult spellings should also be avoided.

If you've researched your book's keywords, consider working one or two keywords into your title, but do not keyword-stuff your title in a way that does not make sense.

SERIES: If your book is part of a series, provide the series name. Pay attention to how each retailer wants series information. Smashwords has a Series Manager section under Metadata Management where the series name and reading order can be provided. Amazon KDP has a series title field and volume field to be filled out during book publishing. The series title must have fewer than 200 characters, and the volume number must be a whole number and not include any text.

The name of your series can be a good place to insert a keyword, but be careful not to keyword-stuff your series name. For example, I used SEO keywords in the names of my series. My Ivy Granger, Psychic Detective urban fantasy series has the keywords "psychic" and "detective" included. My upcoming Whitechapel Paranormal Society Victorian horror series has the keywords "Whitechapel" and "paranormal" included in the series name.

PUBLISHER: The publisher name is the name you used when acquiring your ISBNs.

DESCRIPTION: This is the information that you'd find on the inside flap of a hardcover or the blurb found on the back of a paperback book. Your description's character limit will depend on the retailer. Amazon requires your description be 30 to 4,000 characters in length. NOOK Press allows up to 5,000 characters. iTunes only allows up to 2,000 characters. Some companies, like Smashwords, ask for a short description of up to 400 characters and a long description up to 4,000 characters.

Like with your book's title, do not enter your book's description in ALL CAPS. Do not include review quotes, false claims (NYT Bestseller, Award Winner), retailer names, addresses, phone numbers, and limited-time promotions.

Write a catchy description that will hook readers. Try to include keywords in the description, but do not list keywords separately below the description or mark with hashtags. Some retailers will pull the book if it notes keyword loading. Reading the descriptions of successful books in your genre can give you an idea of what works well.

If you have difficulty writing your description, hire a copywriting professional. If you do write your own description, have it professionally edited or at least read by several beta readers. If readers find grammatical errors and spelling mistakes in your book's description, they will assume that your book is also filled with errors.

If your book has won awards or reached sales milestones like hitting the NYT bestsellers list, include this with your book's description. You should also add award-winning author and/or NYT bestselling author to your author bio.

ISBN: In most cases you have the choice between using a free ISBN provided by the retailer or POD company, or using an ISBN that you own. Remember that a free ISBN will list the retailer or POD company as the publisher on your book's product page. If you want your books to be indistinguishable from traditionally published books, you will need to use your own ISBN.

KEYWORDS AND CATEGORIES: Providing strategic keywords and categories will help increase your book's visibility. Learn more about keywords and categories in the next chapter, **Chapter 13: SEO, Keywords, and BISAC**.

EDITORIAL REVIEWS: Some retailers, like NOOK Press, provide a field for adding editorial reviews during the publishing process. Other retailers, like Amazon, provide an option for adding editorial reviews once the book has been published. We'll cover how to use Amazon's Author Central to add editorial reviews to Amazon product pages once your book goes live.

Editorial reviews should be direct quotes from reliable, professional review sources and must be short in length. Remember to include the review source with the review quote.

CUSTOMER REVIEWS: Customer reviews are different from editorial reviews. Do not quote customer reviews in the editorial review section of your product page. Customer reviews will appear on your product page organically.

AUTHOR BIO: Write your author bio in third person. Include your accomplishments such as books or series written, awards won, and sales milestones such as becoming a NYT bestseller. If you have many books, series, and accomplishments, stick to the highlights. Your author bio should be concise.

AUTHOR PHOTO: In addition to an author bio, most retailers will allow you to add an author photo. Just like with your book cover, use a professional, high quality image. There are many photographers who do author headshots for a reasonable price. If that is not an option, have a friend take a series of photos of you. Keep your author platform in mind when posing for photos, and include props and settings that relate to what you write. Get a second opinion on what photo to use by posting your top picks to your blog or social networks and let your readers choose their favorite.

CREATING: Once you decide on how to describe and categorize your book, you will need to upload the information for your book's retailers. Some retailers allow you to begin your book's setup before you hit publish. Become familiar with each retailer's author dashboard and consider inputting your book's basic information in advance. If you are setting up a pre-order, keep in mind that the data you provide will appear on the product page from the beginning of the pre-order period. If you intend to make your book immediately available, the information will appear on the book's product page as soon as it goes live.

Your book should begin to appear on retail product pages within 1-3 days for ebooks, but may take up to 6 weeks for expanded distribution of print books. Once you hit publish, there may be a period of hours or days in which you cannot access or make changes to your book's metadata.

UPDATING: If the information on your book's product page is incorrect, do not panic. Your book's data may take hours or days to fully populate the product page. Formatting of your product page can also change. Give the retailer time to fully create your book's product page. I have noticed that print book product pages are notorious for taking days for the book's metadata to fully populate the page.

If you have waited and still see errors, you can go into your dashboard for that retailer or the company you are using to distribute to that retailer (Smashwords, Draft2Digital) and make changes. Changes may take days to appear. If you cannot access your book's metadata, or your changes do not appear after 72 hours, contact customer service. The good news is that you have an additional option when publishing to Amazon.

Amazon has created an author portal giving you control over your product pages. Author Central (authorcentral.amazon.com) is a great tool for updating your book's description, adding professional reviews, and maintaining your Amazon author page. In the tutorial later in this chapter, I'll provide step-by-step instructions on how to customize and update your product pages using Author Central.

LINKING FORMATS: Is your book available in more than one format? If so, you will want to link your product pages. Keeping your book title and series name consistent across channels will help retailers. Going into your Author Central account with Amazon and claiming each book format as yours can also help.

There will still be times that a retailer will not realize that each format is a different edition of the same book. If your book product pages for each format do not link, contact customer service.

For example, you can link your book's print edition and Kindle edition. Go to your **KDP** account, click on the **Help** tab, scroll down, and click on the **Contact Us** button in the left sidebar. Make sure to provide the print edition's ISBN and the Kindle edition's ASIN.

When contacting a retailer's customer service provide as much information as you can. I like to include the book title, author name, ISBN/ASINs, and product page URLs. Make helping you as easy as possible. It may seem like common sense, but be polite in your dealings with retailers. Say please and thank you, and never type your request in ALL CAPS. If you are polite, your customer service representative will be more likely to help you.

HOW TO: Amazon controls 70% of the ebook market and over 60% of the online print market. Your book's Amazon product page can showcase your book in all of its formats (Kindle, print, audio) and link to your author page which showcases you and all of your books, including Kindle, print, audio, and all language translations. This easily makes your book's Amazon product page the most important online real estate that you have.

Author Central is your greatest tool for managing your Amazon product page and author page. You can use your Author Central account to add books to your author page, and add editorial reviews and author bio to your book's product page. You can also add, update, and format your book's description.

Log in to **Author Central** (authorcentral.amazon.com, authorcentral.amazon.co.uk, authorcentral.amazon.de, authorcentral.amazon.fr, or authorcentral.amazon.co.jp) and go to the **Books** tab. Note that you need an Author Central account for each country's Amazon store. Click the **Add More Books** button to claim a book as your own.

PRO TIP: If you can't find your book by its title, try searching by ISBN or ASIN. There is also a common glitch that when you hit save, an error message will say you can't add the book at this time. Click save again. This usually works. If it does not, try again later. New books can take a few days to connect to Author Central.

Once your book is added, it will show in your list of books in the **Books** section of your dashboard and on your Amazon author page. There may be a delay before you are able to access and make changes to your book.

Click on your book. If your book is available on Amazon in multiple formats and you have followed the steps above to have those product pages linked, your book will have each format listed under **Editions** in the top right. Select the edition you want to manage. Audible Audio Editions can be viewed, but updating through Author Central is not supported at this time. Inclusion in the AC dashboard is a positive sign that updating may become available in the near future.

One major difference between your book's Kindle and paperback edition is the dashboard interface for adding and updating editorial reviews.

For print editions, you will need to enter each review quote separately. Go to **Review**, click the **Add** button, enter your review quote and include the review source (mandatory), and click **Save**. A new **Review** field will appear below the first. **Repeat** for each quote.

For Kindle editions, enter all of your editorial review quotes into the same box. Go to **Review**, click the **Add** button, enter all review quotes, and click **Save**.

PRO TIP: Never copy and paste a review from Word or from a website. Author Central is very sensitive and will carry over formatting that will wreak havoc on your book's product page formatting. If you must copy and paste information, paste it into **TextEdit** or use another method to strip the text of all formatting.

The **Description** section is located below the **Review** section. Go to **Product Description** and click the **Edit** button. The **Edit Review** window will open. Note that above and to the right of the text box there is a **Compose** tab and an **Edit HTML** tab. The text in the text box will look differently depending on which tab you are currently viewing.

Click the **Compose** tab (the default) and you will see that there are buttons for Bold, Italics, Numbered List, and Bulleted List. Look at other book descriptions in your genre. You may want to **Bold** your tagline or a sentence that highlights your book's awards and achievements. To do so, **highlight/select** the sentence and click the **Bold** button. Click the **Preview** button. Are the correct words in bold? Is your description's line spacing correct? If not correct, click the **Go Back** button. If you approve, click the **Save Changes** button. Clicking the save changes button is the only way your changes will be made on Amazon.

If you know HTML or are willing to learn the basics, you can click on the **Edit HTML** tab to view the HTML for your book's description. Basic HTML tags are allowed. If you are having trouble with Amazon adding large spaces to your book's description, the **Edit HTML** text box is the best place to fix the problem. Remove the extra **Line Break** tags, click the **Compose** tab, and click the **Preview** button. If not correct, click the **Go Back** button. If you approve, click the **Save Changes** button. Clicking the save changes button is the only way your changes will be made on Amazon.

The sections below your book's **Description** (**From the Author**, **From the Inside Flap**, **From the Back Cover**, **About the Author**) are optional. Look at product pages for successful books in your book's genre to see how authors and publishers are using these sections.

CHAPTER 13:
SEO, KEYWORDS, AND BISAC

Understanding SEO, keywords, and BISAC subject codes is essential to aiding your book's discoverability. If you do a quick online search, you'll see that there are millions of published books competing for reader attention. As a fantasy author, for example, you'll be pitting your book against over 1.2 million fantasy books on Amazon alone. This chapter will help you learn what words are important to your book's success and where to use them.

SEO: Search Engine Optimization (SEO) is the process of increasing online visibility. The basic goal of SEO is to drive traffic and improve rankings by pushing your site and content to the top of search engine results. As an author, you want people to be able to find you and your books.

Once you learn SEO, it can be applied to multiple aspects of your book such as title, series name, cover blurb, and product page. SEO can also help improve the visibility of your blog posts, social networking posts, and author bio.

The good news for writers is that the most important SEO tool we have is words. Using the right words makes sites more search engine friendly and can move your book to the top of retailer search results. See the section below on finding the best keywords for you and your books.

Another important tool of SEO is back-links. Back-links are when a webpage other than your own, links back to your website. The more back-links to your site (author website, blog, book product page), the higher search engines will rank your site. If you want your site to appear at the top of search results, you need to encourage back-links.

Back-links often occur when a blogger reviews your book or posts an interview or guest post to their blog and social media sites. Providing ARCs to reviewers, participating in interviews, and writing guest posts are important, but do not forget to provide bloggers and other members of the press with links to your sites. Include your site links on business cards, promotional materials, sell sheets, email signature, press releases, online media kit, and in all direct correspondence with the press. Make it easy for bloggers and other members of the press to add back-links to their articles, reviews, interviews, and guest posts.

PRO TIP: Do not try to game the system. Many companies will try to sell back-links to your site with the claim that it will improve your site's search results, but search engines like Google are skilled at finding and punishing sites that try to cheat their search algorithms. At best, you will have wasted money. At worst, your site may be blacklisted by Google, Bing, or Yahoo. Rely on your site's content and strategic use of keywords rather than paid shortcuts.

KEYWORDS: Keywords are words or short phrases that describe you, your website, or your book. These are the words that readers will use as search terms when performing a search on a search engine like Google, Bing, or Yahoo, or on a retailer like Amazon. For the purposes of this guide, we'll focus on keywords for your book.

Keywords must be relevant and accurately portray your book's content. If a search engine discovers you are trying to cheat the system and load in irrelevant keywords, they can nd will blacklist you. Create a list of terms or phrases that describe your book. Consider your book's setting, character, plot, theme, and tone.

What categories does your book fit into? Add categories and subcategories to your list. These do not need to follow BISAC categories. Think about categories where your book might be shelved in a library or bookstore (romance) and categories or labels that book reviewers might use (paranormal romance, regency romance, contemporary romance) when describing your book.

To find the best keywords for your book, perform a search for books in your genre. Think like a customer. If you wanted to buy a book like yours, what words would you use in an online search? Make a list of the search words that you use. What words are relevant to your book, but have less competition? If there is less competition, your book will appear higher in search results.

When selecting keywords, you will need to find a balance between quantity and quality. You want to increase visibility to stimulate a large quantity of visits, but you also want those visitors to be quality visitors who will be interested in your books. General keywords like fiction or mystery will reach more people. Specific keywords and phrases like female sleuth or spy thriller will target a smaller group of readers.

Some authors already have a built in fan base. Knowing the words that your fans are using to find you can help in creating keywords for your next book. If you have a blog or website, look at what keywords most frequently bring readers to your site. Do the words that drive traffic to your website also apply to your book?

Once you have a preliminary list of keywords, you'll need to test the words on Google Adwords and on Amazon. There are two types of keywords: SEO keywords that will increase traffic from sources outside an online retailer and the keywords that will perform best when a reader is searching within a retailer website.

Google Adwords is the best place to test your SEO keywords. Keyword Planner is a free Google Adwords tool designed to provide statistics and determine how keywords will perform. You will need a Google Adwords account to use the Keyword Planner (adwords.google.com/keywordplanner) tool. Keyword Planner can be used to research keywords and get historical statistics and traffic forecasts. In addition to the free keyword tool, you can run an inexpensive ad with Google Adwords to test your keywords.

Amazon is the best place to test retailer keywords. Go to Amazon and begin a search using your keywords. When entering words into a search, Amazon's auto-complete will suggest keywords. It is important to pay attention to what keywords and phrases Amazon suggests. The top suggestions are the power performers. Note that long-tail keywords currently perform better in Amazon searches than short-tail keywords. These are unwieldy for including in book titles, but long-tail keywords are effective when used as the seven keywords for your product page. We'll discuss short-tail versus long-tail keywords in the HOW TO section below.

Now that you've narrowed down your keywords, begin working your keywords into your title, series name, book description, and author bio. Each retailer will also allow a certain number of keywords to be entered in a keywords field in your book's dashboard. These keywords will become part of your book's product page.

Some retailers, like Amazon, have strict rules about the keywords that may be added in your book's product page from your author dashboard. In the case of Amazon, you are allowed seven words or short phrases and they must adhere to Amazon's keyword policy. Learn more about choosing Amazon keywords in this chapter's HOW TO section. This is crucial to creating your book's Amazon product page which we discuss in **Chapter 12: Retail Product Pages**.

PRO TIP: Amazon allows seven keywords. A common misconception is that this means a book can only have seven words in the keyword section. This is false. Amazon now allows long-tail keywords. Phrases using multiple words are acceptable and count as one keyword.

BISAC: BISAC is an acronym for Book Industry Standards and Communications. The BISAC Subject Headings List, also known as the BISAC Subject Code List, is the industry standard list for subject headings and their nine-character alphanumeric code. These headings and corresponding codes tell people in the book trade the primary and secondary store sections where a book will fit best and sell best, helping with database searching and acting as shelving guides.

Knowing the book industry's headings and codes will help you market your book directly to libraries and retailers and will get your book shelved more quickly. Amazon KDP uses BISAC codes. You will need to select your book's primary and secondary BISAC codes when setting up your book through Amazon KDP. Making the best BISAC code selections will ensure your book is properly categorized, increasing your book's visibility with the right readers and improving customer satisfaction.

The BISAC Subject Headings List has fifty major sections. The list is available free at BISG online (bisg.org/page/BISACsubjectcodes). The first step is to choose the major heading which best describes your book. Click on the major heading to see more specific headings in that category.

EXAMPLE: Let's pretend that your book is a post-apocalyptic novel for young adults. Clicking on the major category Young Adult Fiction will reveal a description of the category and a list of specific categories within Young Adult Fiction. "YAF003000 YOUNG ADULT FICTION / Apocalyptic & Post-Apocalyptic" looks like a good fit for your book. YAF003000 is the BISAC alphanumeric code, YOUNG ADULT FICTION is the major category, and Apocalyptic & Post-Apocalyptic is the more specific categorization which will help libraries and book retailers know where to shelve your book and will help readers discover and purchase your book.

Amazon allows for two BISAC categories. Do not be redundant. If you have already selected Young Adult Fiction > Apocalyptic & Post-Apocalyptic, then do not also select Young Adult Fiction. There are many additional categories to choose from, and providing a second specific category will help your book's visibility.

Some categories have keyword prerequisites on Amazon and Amazon.UK. Additional information on how to access Amazon's special category keyword requirements in the HOW TO section below.

PRO TIP: Include your book's BISAC subject codes on sell sheets. Unlike your Amazon product page, you are not limited to just two codes. On your sell sheets, include all of the BISAC codes that you think best fit your book. Sell sheets are an important tool in marketing your book to libraries and booksellers. You can learn more about sell sheets in **Chapter 16: Bookstores, Libraries, and Sell Sheets**.

HOW TO: Amazon has a keyword policy that restricts what words and phrases can be used. Some BISAC categories also have special keyword requirements on Amazon. Following the tips below will help you avoid punishment by Amazon and can boost your book's placement in Amazon search results.

DO:
- Use Relevant Keywords
- Use Long-Tail Keywords
- Combine Keywords in Logical Order
- Separate Keywords with Commas
- Note Character Limit
- Use 7 Keywords
- Note BISAC Keyword Requirements

DO NOT:
- Variants of Spelling
- Your Title or Author Name
- Other Titles or Author Names
- Subjective Claims of Quality
- Misleading Keywords
- Refer to Temporary Promotion
- Refer to Sales Rank
- Quotation Marks
- Amazon Program Names (KU, KDP)

The most common mistake indie authors make is limiting their seven Amazon keywords to seven actual words. Recent studies show that short-tail keywords, keywords consisting of just one word, do not perform as well as long-tail keywords.

Long-tail keywords are keywords that are made up of multiple words. But these should not be random words lumped together. The keyword phrase should be arranged in logical order. Test your word order by entering words into Amazon's search bar. Amazon's auto-complete will provide popular search word combinations.

Another common mistake is to put your long-tail keywords in quotation marks. Using quotation marks will limit searches to your exact keyword phrase, reducing your book's appearance in search results. Do not use quotation marks, but do separate each keyword or keyword phrase with commas. Commas indicate the break between keywords.

Do not try to increase traffic to your book's product page by being misleading or fraudulent. Relevant keywords will produce the best results and will not risk your page being removed.

There is one more keyword requirement that is extremely important on Amazon. There are keyword prerequisites to being listed in certain categories. The following categories, and all subsequent subcategories, have keyword requirements, including Biographies & Memoirs; Literature & Fiction; Business & Money; Mystery, Thriller, & Suspense; Children's eBooks; Religion & Spirituality; Comics & Graphic Novels; Romance; Erotica; Science Fiction & Fantasy; Health, Fitness, & Dieting; Teen & Young Adult; History; Textbooks; LGBT; and Travel.

Accessing Amazon's category keyword requirements is easy. Go to your **Amazon KDP** account, click **Help**, **Enter Book Information**, and select **Selecting Browse Categories** in the left sidebar. Scroll down and click on your category to get the chart of keyword requirements for listing in that category.

Let's put together what we've learned. Rather than using the short-tail keyword romance, we can use the long-tail keyword romance paranormal shifter. We can change the word order to paranormal romance shifter, since paranormal romance is more logical than romance paranormal. Our keyword is not contained in quotation marks, and is separated from the other six keywords by commas. To be included in the Romance > Paranormal > Werewolves & Shifters category, the words "werewolf" or "shapeshifter" will also need to be used in our keywords.

You are now ready to progress to the next chapter and create your retail product page. Worried about how your keywords will perform? The good news is that Amazon KDP allows you to change your keywords at any time. If you are unhappy with your book's visibility in search results, you can update your keywords. This is a great way to keep up with industry trends and reader preferences.

To update your book's keywords, log in to your **Amazon KDP** account, go to the **Bookshelf** tab, click on the **Edit Button** with three dots beside your book, and select **Edit**

Details. Scroll down to **keywords** and update your book's keywords.

Note that if you are updating keywords on an old book, you may end up with less keywords than you previously had. When I began publishing my books over seven years ago, Amazon KDP had a larger keyword limit and character limit. Changes to those books resulted in having less keywords (the current seven keyword limit), but changing to higher quality keywords still improved book visibility. No matter how old the book, it's never too late to improve its performance.

CHAPTER 14: ADVERTISING AND PRICE PROMOTIONS

Advertising is an important part of book marketing, but can quickly eat up your marketing budget. Popular ad services include Google Ads, Facebook ads, and BlogAds. A smart strategy is to use advertising to enhance a marketing campaign, rather than run book ads alone. Ads can boost the signal on a book release, giveaway, or sale.

Price promotions are the most effective form of book marketing campaign. Lowering a book's price for a limited time creates a sense of urgency, appeals to bargain shoppers, and makes the book more affordable to readers who may not be able to buy your book at its regular price. Price promotions that are combined with a successful advertising campaign will improve a book's ranking, make a book hit bestsellers lists and charts, increase visibility on retailers, drive sales to all books in a series for long-tail profits, gain new readers, and get new reviews.

In this chapter, we'll give tips on the best paid and free advertising sites to use for running a price promotion ad, strategies on how to submit and get accepted to those sites, and the rules and limitations to keep in mind to maximize the number of promotions you can run each year.

Price Promotion Advertising Sites:
Sites that advertise price promotions vary in price, reach, effectiveness (ROI), and long-tail sales impact. I've ranked popular sites into four tiers based on overall effectiveness with Tier 1 being the most effective.

At the moment, Bookbub (bookbub.com) rules Tier 1 by being far and above the greatest way to advertise a price promotion. Bookbub has millions of email subscribers and

Facebook followers, targeted genre-specific reader lists, and the readers on those lists are hungry for book bargains, but Bookbub is the most expensive and has notoriously strict submission rules.

A good strategy is to submit to Bookbub, but do not count 100% on getting a Bookbub ad. Submit to Tier 2 and Tier 3 sites, and use Tier 4 sites to fill in any scheduling gaps or combine with other ads for a small boost.

Tier 1:
Bookbub

Tier 2:
Ereader News Today (ENT)
Free Booksy

Tier 3:
Bargain Booksy
BKnights Fiverr
Book Barbarian
Books Butterfly
Book of the Day
Booksends
Free Kindle Books and Tips (FKBT)
Fussy Librarian
Robin Reads

Tier 4:
Armadillo Ebooks
Awesomegang
Book Basset
Book Lemur
Book Lovers Heaven
Bookraid
Bookscream
Choosy Bookworm
Dealer's Room
Digital Book Today
Discount Bookman
Ebookasaurus

Ebookhounds
Genre Crave
Genre Pulse
Goddess Fish
My Book Cave
Pretty Hot
Price Dropped Books
ReadCheaply
Reading Deals
Reddit

PRO TIP: Don't forget to utilize your mailing list and social media. Send an email to your mailing list, make a blog post, and make social media announcements on the first day of your price promotion. Pay to boost social media posts or take out a Facebook ad to promote your book's price drop. If running a Facebook ad or boosting a Facebook post, select the demographics that best match your readers (age, gender, interests) and the sales promotion (countries where the book will be on sale).

Submission Tips:
There's no super power to use to get approved by a top tier advertising site, but there are ways to improve your odds. Submissions are rejected or accepted based on:
- Book Cover
- Book Description
- Number of Reviews
- Review Rating
- First in Series
- Book Length
- Genre Competition
- Sale Price
- Ad Date Flexibility

Make sure that your book has a quality, eye-catching book cover that is suitable for its genre. Replace blurry images with higher resolution files, and update a bad cover with a custom cover by a professional book cover designer.

Check that the book description is interesting, well written, and is free of errors. Spelling and grammatical errors in a book's description reflect poorly on the book and will result in a rejection. Include the most impressive awards you or your books have won and bestsellers lists you or your book have achieved.

The minimum number of reviews and the book's review rating that is required for each advertising site varies greatly, and some, like BookBub, do not post their minimum review requirements, but having more reviews and high star rating will always improve your odds. If your book has less than twenty-five reviews or a star rating lower than 4.0, you may be limited to the low tier advertising sites. Improve your chance of ad acceptance and increase your book's sales by using the tips in **Chapter 11: Book Reviews and ARC Reviews** to run a successful book review campaign.

PRO TIP: Use caution when running free and permafree deals. Free will drive volume sales, but keep an eye on your book's review rating. The price of a book can sometimes influence its perceived quality. If you start receiving a large number of negative reviews when your book is priced at free, consider changing your book's price or sale price to $0.99.

Many sites, such as Book Barbarian and FKBT, will only accept stand-alone books or the first book in a series. Readers prefer deals on the first book in a series and ad sites must maintain and grow their lists by keeping readers happy. BookBub will occasionally run an ad for later books in a series (they ran a deal in 2016 for Ghost Light the second novel in the Ivy Granger series), but your best chance of getting accepted is to submit the first book in the series. The good news is that sales for all books in a series are five times greater when the price promotion is run on the first book in the series.

Most top tier sites will only accept full-length novels. Improve your submission odds by running a deal on a novel. If you are running a price promotion on short fiction such as a novella, narrow your submissions to sites that have run deals on novellas in the past, such as Armadillo Ebooks, BKnights, Booklover's Heaven, Bookscream, Discount Bookman Ebookasaurus, and Fussy Librarian.

The majority of advertising sites separate their reader lists by genre. When you submit your book, you have to select the genre to advertise to. Some categories have more competition than others. This competition can impact whether your book gets accepted and how well your book's price promotion performs. If your book fits multiple categories, experiment to find your best fit for each advertising site.

Choose your sale price carefully. If your book is not deeply discounted from its regular price, your ad submission may be rejected. Most sites, including BookBub, will only accept ads for a deal price of free or at least 50% off the book's original price. The lowest price books, those priced at free and $0.99 will get priority since they will appeal more to the advertiser's readers. You'll make a smaller royalty percentage, but sales are 75% higher for books priced at $0.99 than at $2.99, and that download volume is what sites like BookBub and ENT are interested in.

Be flexible with your promotion start and end dates. A promotion with a thirty day window will be easier to fit into the advertiser's schedule than a promotion with a two day window. With top tier sites, offer to be flexible within their thirty day schedule and/or run your price promotion for more than three days. Running a promotion for more than three days makes working you into their schedule easier and is more likely to drive sales to the rest of your series.

PRO TIP: If you get rejected for one sale price or genre category, try a lower price or different genre category for your next submission.

Timing Strategies:
Many top tier and even some bottom tier price promotion advertising sites have restrictions on the frequency of ads run. These restrictions are on the individual book and on the author. Consider each site's restrictions when creating your book marketing plan for the year.

Most sites will not feature any book more than once per month. As of today, Bookbub, Book Raid, Ereader News Today, ReadCheaply, and Robin Reads have additional site restrictions on the frequency of books. BookBub will not feature the same book again for 6 months. Robin Reads and

ENT will not feature the same book again for 90 days. ReadCheaply will not feature the same book again for 4 months. Book Raid will not feature the same book again for 8 weeks.

As of today, BookBub, ReadCheaply, Book Basset have site restrictions on the frequency of authors. BookBub, ReadCheaply, Book Basset will not feature the same author more than once every 30 days.

PRO TIP: Rules and policies change over time, so check each site's policy page or FAQ page for updates.

Use a calendar or calendar app to schedule when your price promotions will run and when you need to submit to each site. Adjustments to your plan can be made based on submission rejections and acceptances.

PRO TIP: BookBub also has a policy regarding the timing of your book's price fluctuations that impacts how you plan your book marketing. BookBub requires that the book not have been on sale for a price lower than the BookBub deal price in the 90 days leading up to the promotion, and that the book not have been reduced to the deal price for more than a total of 14 days in the last 90 days. So even if you want to run a price promotion and advertise it on other sites that price fluctuation can impact your ability to get approved with BookBub. The one exception is for free books.

Change Book Price:
Once you've set the dates for your price promotion to begin and your ads are scheduled and approved, you need to make a plan to lower your book's price. Note that if you are traditionally published you will not have access to your book's retailer dashboards, so an arrangement will need to be made with your publisher in advance.

For indie authors, I advise making the changes 48 hours before your price promotion is scheduled to begin. If running a free promotion and you've lined up advertising on top tier sites, make changes 72 hours in advance to give Amazon time to price match your book. If your book is not at the agreed upon sale price on the day of your ad, the ad will not run and you may be blacklisted with the advertising site and banned from submitting future promotions.

If lowering the price to free, lower the price on Amazon to 99 cents. Amazon is more likely to price match to free when a book's price is set at 99 cents and at the 35% royalty rate. If Amazon still does not price match your book to free, contact KDP customer service and provide proof that your book is free on all other sites by including direct links to your book on retailers such as Barnes & Noble, Kobo, and iTunes. When corresponding with Amazon customer service, always be polite, be clear, and include your book's title and ASIN.

PRO TIP: Whenever changing a book's price back to its original price, change the price on Amazon last. Amazon has a price matching policy. If you try to raise the price on Amazon while the price is still at the retail price on other sites, Amazon will see the lower price on other retailers and will not raise the price. Change the price on all other retailers first. Check retailer sites to verify price change. When the price has updated on all other retailers, change the price on Amazon.

CHAPTER 15: BUILDING A NEWSLETTER MAILING LIST

A mailing list is a powerful, direct marketing tool that allows you to communicate directly with readers who are interested in your books. A mailing list can be used to send emails and/or snail mail. The most popular use of an author mailing list is for sending an email newsletter.

PRO TIP: Never buy a list or add people who have not voluntarily subscribed to your list.

Select an email marketing tool such as MailChimp (mailchimp.com), ActiveCampaign, AWeber, Benchmark Email, or Campaign Monitor. Prices vary depending on the features you need and the size of your mailing list.

If you can't afford using one of these apps, you can paste your email list into the bcc field of a basic email and send a monthly or weekly email to your readers. Note that there are many risks involved with sending your own emails, including being marked as spam and having your email blocked. Authors who manually send their own emails will need to create their own signup form and maintain integrating form information to update their list. I recommend using Google Docs forms due to their ability to easily send form information into an organized spreadsheet.

You will need to build, maintain, and grow your list over time. You can encourage new sign ups at in-person events and online. At events, print out a signup sheet and put it on your signing table or vendor table. For gaining new subscribers online, put a call-to-action to sign up for your mailing list on your website, blog, and social media pages.

PRO TIP: Facebook pages offer a call-to-action button. Add a newsletter signup button to your Facebook page(s) to grow your mailing list. Select sign up as the type of call-to-action button, or you can add the button from your newsletter service site (for integrated sites) such as Mailchimp. If adding the button through Mailchimp, you need to setup Facebook integration first. Check Mailchimp Help for more information on this.

Giveaways are also a great way to grow your list. Make signing up for your mailing list an entry option and watch your list grow. More information on how to run a successful giveaway in **Chapter 9: Giveaways**.

PRO TIP: Do not try to embed a giveaway form in your email newsletter. The javascript will likely be disabled and might be flagged as malicious code. Instead, run the giveaway on your website or blog and in your newsletter provide a link to where the giveaway is taking place.

Giving away a free book or exclusive short story to new subscribers is another great way to grow your list. You can automate the process using MailChimp or Book Funnel, or you can track new sign ups and manually send their free read as an attachment, a Smashwords coupon code, or a link to the free read.

PRO TIP: No matter how you collect subscriber information, remember to periodically download and backup your list.

Once you build your list, you'll need to keep readers interested and engaged. If you only send links to buy your books, they'll unsubscribe. They might even report you for spam.
Instead, write entertaining, informative posts. Provide highlights from your recent author events, book news, and provide links to giveaways. Include photos from your events, but do not upload large images that will slow down your newsletter's load time.

Before sending out your newsletter, have a beta reader look it over, or hire an editor. Send a preview copy to your own email address, and test how it looks on your computer and on a mobile device. Is it easy to navigate? Does it load quickly? Do the links work and direct to the proper website? Readers expect quality, well written, error-free posts, and working links.

PRO TIP: Include social follow buttons in your newsletter to drive traffic to your social media sites and to encourage reader engagement.

CHAPTER 16: SELL SHEETS

A sell sheet is a single page document that provides all of the information about your book. You can think of it like a visually appealing combination of a press release and a book resume. Sell sheets are a useful tool for marketing your book to consumers and to wholesalers like bookstores and libraries.

Information:
There is no right way to format a sell sheet, but there is information that should be included. Every sell sheet should provide:
- Book Title
- Author Name
- Book Description
- Formats
- Price
- ISBN
- BISAC Categories
- Distributor Info
- Your Contact Info

A sell sheet should always include a full-color thumbnail image of your book's cover. If printing your own, you may need to lighten the image for it to print well. Make sure to use a high-resolution image.

Whether you use portrait or landscape orientation, put your book's title in large print at the top of the document. Include the author name, a short book description, the formats available, and the price per format.

Providing an ISBN makes it easy for consumers, retailers, and libraries to search for your book in any database. Genre categories are helpful for consumers, but BISAC categories are extremely helpful to bookstores and libraries because it guides them to where the book will be shelved.

Let them know where the book is available. For bookstores and libraries this includes wholesale distributors. Don't forget to include your contact email and a link to your website.

Design:

The design of your sell sheet is up to you. Get creative. Try to match your author brand or pull color and font styles from your book cover. Limit fonts to three font styles and make sure that text is clear and legible.

When printing, print in full-color and use high quality paper. You can pay to have copies made at stores like Staples, Kinkos, and Office Max, or order flyers from online retailers like Vistaprint.

Distribute:

Include your sell sheets in your digital media kits, provide to potential narrators and translators, bring to signings and events, and mail or hand deliver to bookstores and libraries.

PRO TIP: Keep one or two sets of sell sheets in pristine condition while traveling with plastic slip covers or sheet protectors. These also work great for saving sheets from dirty hands and coffee spills. Standard 8.5 x 11 inch sell sheets fit in the magazine size slip covers sold at comic book and collectible stores. You can also get clear sheet protectors that have a three-hole punched edge for keeping in a binder. Avery makes a variety of affordable sheet protectors. Make sure that covers are acid free for long-term storage.

CHAPTER 17:
BOOK SIGNINGS AND CONVENTIONS

In-person events are a great way to build lasting relationships with readers. They are also a great way to increase visibility for you and your books and to network with other publishing industry professionals.

Events can be expensive. Consider travel, lodging, food, registration, and supply costs, and ask yourself what your goal is for attending. Common expenses to budget for are:
- Taxi
- Tips (Waiter/Porter/Driver)
- Airfare/Train/Bus
- Luggage Fees
- Shipping Fees
- Hotel
- Food
- Registration Fee
- Vendor Fee
- Electric/Wi-Fi Fee
- Program Ad Fee
- Welcome Bag Fee
- Promotional Items
- Books
- Clothing*

*Clothing is not a tax deduction, but it can be a very real business expense. Some events, especially awards banquets, black tie dinners, and masquerade balls, have a dress code. Plan and budget accordingly.

Goals:
Are you there to make money, network, or gain exposure? Setting clear goals will help you choose an event that's right for you.

If your goal is to make money, you will need premium vendor space, professional signage, and quality inventory. Most authors do not make a large profit at events, but there's often an online boost in sales immediately after events. Encourage sales with a friendly demeanor and entice buyers with candy, free swag, and games of chance. Authors who are successful vendors usually have a gimmick for bringing customers to their table.

PRO TIP: An empty table is uninviting. Ask a friend or an assistant to come to your table and "seed the pot" by signing up for your mailing list and playing one of your games of chance. You can even take turns doing this with other authors to help each other out. When attendees see that something is happening at your table, they'll come to investigate.

If your goal is networking and/or exposure, apply to be on programming. Speaking on a panel, hosting a party, or doing a reading will get you in front of an audience and give you a chance to demonstrate your professionalism, unique knowledge, and fun personality.

PRO TIP: Always carry pens and business cards at events. It's also helpful to bring a custom tote bag to carry a print copy of your latest book, a set of sell sheets, and a handful of promotional swag.

Selling Books:
Some events allow authors to sell their books, and some allow the sale of other items like book related t-shirts, jewelry, and tote bags. Check to see if any sales are allowed, what items can be sold, the hours that any vendor space is open, if there is a vendor fee, how large the vendor booth space is, if electricity and/or Wi-Fi is included or can be purchased, what furniture or backdrops are provided, table size and if it's shared with another author, what signage is allowed, if food or drink is allowed in the vendor area, if an additional chair and badge are provided for an assistant, and if any additional permits and/or sales tax documentation must be filed for before the event.

If you plan to make sales, bring a supply of small bills for making change. A locking bag for cash, a calculator, pen, notepad, and a receipt book are helpful. I also highly recommend signing up for Square or PayPal so that you can accept credit cards as payment. Most convention center ATMs run out of money midway through an event, so do not count on customers having access to cash.

The good news is that Square, my preferred payment tool, is easy to use and can be run with the free app on most phones and tablets. You can enter cards manually with the app, get the free card reader, and/or purchase the combination Apple Pay touchless device and chip card reader. Square processes the transactions, can email a receipt to the customer, sends you sales information, and deposits your money into your bank account.

To make the process even faster, add your items to your Square store before the event. Then you won't need to keep entering prices. Just tap the item and it goes into the shopping cart and will be listed on your sales records and on the customer's receipt. You can even set it up to keep inventory for you.

PRO TIP: Even marketing super heroes can get sick, hungry, or need to freshen up. Bring a survival kit containing breath mints, bottled water, protein or granola bars, dental floss, headache and allergy remedies, pocket tissues, and hand sanitizer.

BOOK MARKETING CHECKLIST

I use lists to help keep on track with my publishing and marketing tasks. I've compiled a to-do list that may come in handy during your publishing journey.

- Build and Maintain Author Platform
- Blog Weekly
- Post to Social Media Daily
- Run Monthly Giveaways
- Send Monthly Newsletter
- Schedule Price Promotions
- Schedule Blog Tours
- Schedule Book Signings and Conventions
- Order Books
- Order Promotional Items
- Update Media Kit
- Update Website
- Update Social Media
- Write Books!

Feel free to customize your checklist. The checklist above is a basic guideline intended as a reminder of tasks to complete and options to consider, taking you one step, leap, and bound closer to becoming a bestseller.

BOOK MARKETING RESOURCES

Need a quick reference to the helpful book marketing resources that we have covered? Visit these online sites to learn more about the topics discussed in this book. For a more comprehensive list of author resources with active, up-to-date links, visit the Resources for Authors page at www.EJStevensAuthor.com.

- Amazon KDP
- Author Central
- Bewitching Book Tours
- BISAC
- Blogger/Blogspot
- BlueHost
- BookBub
- Book Funnel
- Buffer
- Creative Market
- Crowdfire
- Ebates
- Facebook
- Go Daddy
- Google Plus
- GotPrint
- Hootesuite
- InkSlinger PR
- Instagram
- Kindle Boards
- LinkedIn
- MailChimp
- National Pen
- Pinterest
- Print Runner
- Pump Up Your Book
- PureTextuality PR

- Rafflecopter
- Smashwords
- Sprout Social
- Square Reader
- Tweetdeck
- Twitter
- VistaPrint
- Wisestamp
- WordPress
- Xpresso Tours
- YouTube

Grab your cape. It's time to be a book marketing hero!

WAS THIS BOOK HELPFUL?

Did you find this book helpful? If this book has made your publishing journey easier, please consider writing a review.

Reviews are the single most powerful way to help the book and the author. If you would like to see more Super Simple Quick Start Guides, please leave a review and share with friends and colleagues.

Thank you.

Looking to independently publish a bestseller? Check out the Super Simple Quick Start Guide to Self-Publishing by E.J. Stevens.

ABOUT THE AUTHOR

E.J. Stevens is the bestselling, award-winning author of the IVY GRANGER, PSYCHIC DETECTIVE urban fantasy series, the SPIRIT GUIDE young adult series, the HUNTERS' GUILD urban fantasy series, and the WHITECHAPEL PARANORMAL SOCIETY Victorian Gothic horror series. She is known for filling pages with quirky characters, bloodsucking vampires, psychotic faeries, and snarky, kick-butt heroines. Her novels are available worldwide in multiple languages.

BTS Red Carpet Award winner for Best Novel, SYAE finalist for Best Paranormal Series, Best Novella, and Best Horror, winner of the PRG Reviewer's Choice Award for Best Paranormal Fantasy Novel, Best Young Adult Paranormal Series, Best Urban Fantasy Novel, and finalist for Best Young Adult Paranormal Novel and Best Urban Fantasy Series.

When E.J. isn't at her writing desk, she enjoys dancing along seaside cliffs, singing in graveyards, and sleeping in faerie circles. E.J. currently resides in a magical forest on the coast of Maine where she finds daily inspiration for her writing. Connect with E.J. on her Website www.EJStevensAuthor.com.

www.ingramcontent.com/pod-product-compliance
Lightning Source LLC
Chambersburg PA
CBHW070643050426
42451CB00008B/290